The Path Leads Here

How to live mindfully in a busy wor

Simon Michaels

Dedication:

This book is dedicated to Lama Jangchub Reid,
with heartfelt thanks for pointing the way.

Printed in the United Kingdom
First Edition, 2018
ISBN 78-1-78926-465-4
Published through Ingram Spark

CONTENTS

Preface

Why did I write this book?

I worked for many years as a consultant, first in environmental planning then as a business advisor in food supply chains. Like many people, I was anxious about getting the work done on time and well enough,  and keeping a steady flow of income. There were often difficulties in relationships with managers or staff, and I often felt under-valued and unmotivated.

Whilst I made a living, life was just not satisfying and the dissatisfaction was spilling over into my social life. I blamed everything but myself for how I felt. Then I was made redundant from a senior position. It was a real shock, and I realised that I needed to re-evaluate my whole approach to work. I became self-employed and started to get creative.

At about this time, I started meditating. The more I practised, the more I realised that my stress at work was easing off. It was not that the external stress factors were any less; I just took it less personally, kept a wider perspective, and was more tolerant. As a result, I became more at ease, more confident, and more resilient. My work improved, and so did my interactions with colleagues and clients.

With more confidence in my values, and feeling more enlivened, I helped establish several ethical enterprises and have now advised over 150 businesses, government agencies, third sector organisations and local authorities.

At home, my practice has been a critical support for some challenging family issues, teaching me how to bring tolerance and love into personal difficulties; and of course, I'm still learning!

After about 12 years of personal practice I trained, and started to teach, mindfulness.

So I've now brought together these two strands – the business advice and mindfulness, into my training company, *Mindful Work*. I help organisations to reduce employee stress, thus improving productivity and workplace happiness.

Whilst my training delivery is secular, practical and business-focused, it has solid foundations. I have over 20 years meditation training in the Buddhist tradition, and in 2017 I was ordained in the lineage of Namgyal Rinpoché. This ordination is in effect a life-long commitment to work for the benefit all beings, and to follow a code of ethical conduct.

I meditate every day and attend regular long retreats, including teachings from Tibetan masters such as Mingur Rinpoché, and I try my best to integrate my values and kindness into everyday actions.

So, my personal journey in mindfulness has taken a route I did not expect. It has helped me though difficult times, enriched my daily life enormously and put everything into perspective. I want to share that with as many people as possible.

How to use this book

This book is a collection of essays, many of which first appeared as blog articles on my website or in the Huffington Post.

They progress from generic reflections to more focused ways to apply the wisdom of mindfulness in daily life. Towards the end are some simple practice guides.

Feel free to dip in to the articles in any order, and take the time to reflect on them in terms of your own life.

However, don't think that by reading, watching videos and dipping into mindfulness apps in a random way you will make a real and lasting difference. It may be interesting and informative, but real and lasting change comes only with regular, sustained practise.

Start with an 8-week course, and then find a way to keep the practice going. There are some 'techniques' around that will be useful, but you've spent decades creating the edifice that you call 'me' and it will take years to permanently reshape it. Don't expect a quick fix.

But it is worth the effort. The prize is enjoying and finding more meaning in life, in each moment, rather than waiting and striving for it all to come together at some point in the future.

There are two things I want to say before you read on.

The first is that mindfulness practice is, and should be, simple. Don't overcomplicate it or try to think your way into it. Just allow yourself to be informed by direct (especially sensory) experience.

3

The second point I want to make is that all of us, without exception, have a clear, calm, spacious baseline nature of mind. Okay, there may be a lot of junk in there obscuring this truth. But you will discover your own sense of calm spaciousness at some point, and when you get even the smallest glimpse of it, you will be inspired to seek more.

The path leads here

Whatever paths and spiritual journeys we may take, the only destination is right here, right now. The answer to our quest for understanding is right in front of our face, if only we could see it.

This is the great secret. It's so simple that we don't notice it. It's like the story of the fish:

One day, a fish was swimming around, much like every other day. He did his chores, ate, swam with the shoal, cheekily dipped a fin at an attractive she-fish, and opened his gills to catch the oxygen, as usual. This day, everything was calm, and his mind was still and open. Quite suddenly he noticed something that changed everything - yet changed nothing at all. He noticed the water.

In the same way, there comes a point in meditation practice when we realise that Awareness exists beyond 'my' awareness, and that it is has always been present. When this insight comes, life transforms. Nothing changes. We still have to get up, deal with family, work, breathe, eat, go to the loo, sleep. There are still bad times and good times, life and death, mediocre and amazing coffees. At the same time our perspective alters, and that changes everything. We know that we are no longer, and never have been, separate from Existence itself - an unchanging field of infinite possibility.

When this becomes apparent, we understand that everything we perceive, feel and think is no more than a temporary appearance in the mind. And that our mind has a space-like, infinite, non-judging and timeless quality.

Happily, this realisation is not difficult to come by. We just have to create the right conditions and one day, the truth quite unexpectedly appears. The core conditions for its discovery are to be in a relaxed, yet alert state and to take the approach that it's not about 'me'.

Right now, as you read this, you can touch on this realisation. Consider your thoughts; notice that between each thought there is a gap. Or look for the gap between your in-breath and out-breath. Catch the feeling of this gap. It has no 'me' to it. It is simply a gap. It has no agenda, and it is unchanging. Now, try to rest your awareness in that gap, simply staying present to the spacious quality of this moment.

'Mindfulness' is the term that's used today for the practice of 'staying with' this awareness.

When we stay present with mindful attention to this ever present awareness, our perspective changes, suffering reduces, and life feels better.

The paths we take in our spiritual journeys will be different for you and for me, but all the paths lead back here.

This precious life

Live now. What are you waiting for?

Look around as if this might be your last day on Earth. Listen as if it might be the last day you hear. Take in the scent of the next flower you find as if you might never smell another. Savour the sweetness of the next fruit you eat as if you may lose the ability to taste tonight. Open up to the touch of another person's skin as if you might never hold anyone's hand again.

We don't know when we'll lose our senses, but one thing is certain: sooner or later we will lose it all. We have this precious gift of being alive, conscious and aware. Just knowing that, and realising the fragility of our health and life, gives us every reason for simple celebration, in every moment.

Of course, life and its challenges distract us. We might go for days or weeks wrapped up in our problems and busy-ness. Days or weeks can pass without the delight that simply being alive can bring.

We don't need a bigger house, a faster car, more sex, a better job, or more zeros at the end of our bank statement to appreciate this simple joy in being alive. It's right here, within you. It is accessible in any moment - like now... and now... and now...

How to wake up and feel good

It is common to release a huge burst of stress hormones within minutes after waking. This can affect us for the whole day. The stress hormone cortisol, for example, is very persistent in the bloodstream. So, it's really useful to get the day off on the right track from the first moment. I've had some personal challenges to cope with in my life, some quite recently. What I'm about to share has helped me through these difficult times.

The first moments of consciousness on waking follow a particular pattern. First of all, there's a kind of innocent, open quality – similar to when you're staying away from home, and for a second or two you can't think where you are. This is actually a great moment to tune in to our naturally 'unformatted' consciousness.

The second thing that happens is that we remember who we are and all our problems can come flooding back in. We may replay internal conversations and fantasies from the night before, or recall a stressful situation we've been (or might go) through.

The third thing that arises upon waking, within a second or less, is the emotional response to all that mental confusion. It can be overwhelming. So we need a powerful practice to counteract the negativity and the stress that can result – and we need to deploy it really quickly.

So here is my formula:

1) **Gratitude**. Think of one thing you are thankful for. It can be as simple as waking up safe and warm, with food in the fridge. Recognise how much we take for granted. For example, your body's systems have kept you breathing without any conscious effort all night, and your blood's pH level has been maintained perfectly, all by itself. Our bodies truly are miraculous.

2) **Get perspective.** Ask yourself this question: 'Am I happy to be alive?' Even if you have problems, or are suffering anxiety or depression, are you nevertheless grateful to experience this life as a conscious human being? This question helps me realise that whatever difficulties are present, they are temporary and in a state of constant change, that it's all just 'stuff'. The bigger picture is that I'm actually okay, I just have stuff to deal with. Your answer to the question, 'Am I happy to be alive?' will probably be 'yes'. If your answer is 'no', however, get help – you're probably suffering acute anxiety or depression and you may not have the resources to get out of it by yourself. And that's ok too.

3) **Get up and move.** If you feel stuck mentally, the body feels it too. You can, however, reverse the whole thing by moving your body. Yoga, exercise, a brisk walk or a run, can be hugely effective, partly due to the well-documented dopamine release. If you are indoors, opening the window will help, but ideally get outside, into nature if possible or just the local park. While you are there, use all your senses take in your environment and make this sensory experience the focus of your attention.

Hooray! It's hopeless.

Nothing is certain or reliably the same. So where does that leave us with finding joy in the things we value?

Well oddly enough, it's exactly in the knowledge that everything changes all the time that we can take some comfort and, ultimately, find freedom and bliss.

One of the core foundations of Buddhist philosophy is *impermanence*. The theory goes that as every thing is assembled from components, at some stage it must fall apart again. Some things disassemble pretty quickly, like the mayflies whose adult life does not even last 24 hours. Mountain ranges take millions of years to break up, but they too will eventually erode into the sea bed. We see things in relation to our own concept of time and in terms of a human life span, but that's only one viewpoint.

Also, to take this further, because we are assembled from atoms like carbon and hydrogen, and fed by a food system that starts with sun and rain, and housed in fired clay bricks, etc., we are not really independent, but just a lump in the general soup of life. So we're all connected and inter-dependent. And we wouldn't be here if the distribution of the soup's ingredients wasn't changing all the time.

Lots of change takes place without us appreciating it too, like the tens of thousands of red blood cells in our bodies that die and are replaced every second. In fact all our body parts get entirely replaced, at different rates, and none longer than seven years. If you took a microscope to your house, you'd see the walls crumbling, ever so slightly.

Yet most of the time we live as if we and the other people and things around us, were pretty much fixed. So when something goes wrong, like getting cancer, or losing our job, or the pension scheme going belly-up, we get a shock.

In fact most of our stress and worry comes from either not wanting things to change, yet they do; or from wanting things to change in a particular way, yet they don't. We're either clinging on for dear life, or trying to avoid what we fear. This takes up energy and can lead to bad behaviours, like greed and hatred.

If everything is going really well for you just now, that's great, but don't get smug; it won't last.

So before you reach for the hemlock, I better move on to why this is good news.

Well first of all there's the opposite scenario to the smug one; if everything is in turmoil and going pear-shaped, that too will change. Sometimes people need to hit rock bottom before they can start to re-build their life. We learn most about life when things go wrong. And even if we're just a bit depressed and stuck, it's inevitable that it will change. Nothing, absolutely nothing, can stay the same.

Well, actually one thing does not change. And that's the potential for change. Out of that soup of life, there are unlimited permutations. Just about anything can happen. When we tap into that potentiality, we flourish. I believe that the really great people we know (not just the public figures but people we most admire), the people who seem supercharged and amazingly creative, or especially kind, can only do what they do by tapping into that unlimited potentiality.

Corporate coach Jamie Smart helps top executives tune-in to this deeper intelligence:

"..many of the most desirable qualities people struggle to 'develop' (such as intuition, resilience, creativity, motivation, confidence and even leadership) are actually innate, emergent properties of an uncluttered mind."

We have a choice in our lives: stay small and stuck because we're fearful of change, or embrace it fully and see where it takes us. If you're honest, where are you on this spectrum? *Nelson Mandela*, quoting *Marianne Williamson*, had this to say about it:

"Our deepest fear is not that we are inadequate. Our deepest fear is that we are powerful beyond measure. It is our light, not our darkness that most frightens us. We ask ourselves, Who am I, to be brilliant, gorgeous, talented, and fabulous? Actually, who are you not to be? You are a child of God. Your playing small does not serve the world."

When we meditate, and stay mindfully attentive, we get to see how we are driven by all kinds of fear of change. We can also begin to drop those fears because we get to experience the underlying, creative, and joyful energy that is our birthright. Our practice helps us gradually gain more confidence in this aspect of human capacity, and to gradually lose our fear of change. Our lives can become more meaningful, more exciting, and we can give more back.

Doing and Being

One of the key features at the core of mindfulness, is being *in the present moment.* What does this actually mean?

You could say that we are always in the moment, because that's where we live our lives. However, we keep ourselves so busy and distracted, and spend so much time thinking about things that have happened, or things that may happen in the future, that we are rarely living fully in the now.

One proof of this is when we do things on *autopilot.* For example, how often have you driven from A to B, but on the way been thinking about any number of things, without really concentrating on the driving; your body just seems to take over and do it while your mind is somewhere else.

At work, in particular, we make ourselves busy and even take pride in the fact that we don't have a moment to stop. Working long hours, taking work home, and generally playing the busyness game reduces effectiveness at work. It also creates serious heath risks. We 'relax' from all this pressure by going to the gym, watching a movie, checking social media, or drinking ourselves into torpor. We never really stop for a moment. This is 'Doing' mode.

On the other hand, most of us have had experiences when time just seemed to stand still. This happens particularly in nature when we become immersed in, say, looking at a wonderful sunset, or the panorama from the top of a mountain. Words and thoughts are not required to feel the power of the moment.

It's good to simply take a break from the busyness and all the thinking, from time to time. This quiet attention is 'Being' mode.

'Being' is time out, but it's not time wasted. Simply giving yourself time to recharge and recalibrate has positive ramifications on health and wellbeing. It is also in these quiet moments of calm presence that creativity and insight blossom.

Gradually, Being becomes more and more natural. It is possible to dwell in this state of calm presence within all our daily activities.

We are all connected

We tend to think of ourselves as separate and unique.

But we're much more alike than different. We all breathe the oxygen exhaled by the plants, we eat food that started as a seed that was planted and harvested by a farmer who may be on the other side of the world. We share 99.9% of DNA with our neighbour, and 92% with mice. Even 'our' human body is really an ecosystem; up to 90% of the cells in our body are not human.

In the same way that Lovelock's Gaia hypothesis helped scientists and philosophers to envisage the Earth as a complex, inter-relating unit, so we can choose to view our community of fellow beings as the tip of the iceberg of humanity, supported by a miraculous, hidden web of biological inter-dependencies.

The paper this is printed on was made from wood pulp, so here is the tree. The tree grew in sunlight, rain and soil, so here is the forest. The tree was cut, the wood pulped and the paper made by people, so here they are. In any one thing around you, or in a grain of sand, the whole universe is present and inter-connected.

It's really easy to think we're separate, whilst in reality we depend on all kinds of other people and things. If you have any doubt about this, think 'conditionality'; for example, is your health conditional on the food supply chain and on the availability of water?

When we recognise and thank the people and the support around us, everyone feels better.

Gratitude

Thank you Virgin Trains for transporting me across the country as I write this, and Apple for my wonderful Macbook Pro. Thank you Nick at the market for the amazing apple I'm munching, and for the rain and sun and apple cultivar breeders.

All that gratitude makes me feel good. The potential to give thanks for whatever supports us is limitless, yet mostly we take it all for granted.

You can try this for yourself. As soon as you wake up, start finding things to be thankful for. The comfort of the bed, the quiet time you've had to sleep, your partner not snoring for a while, the near perfect mix of oxygen and other gases which has been silently keeping you alive all night, the nice rug under your feet as you swing your legs out of bed, that you can feel your feet, and so on.

Your list could continue endlessly. How about thanks too, for the teenager barging past you with a grunt (all is clearly normal), the traffic jam (that gives us a minute of time to practise mindful presence), the sneer from your boss when you are late (which you counter with a smile), the angry-sounding email from a client (you wonder if they are ok). When we get challenged, we have an opportunity to learn how to become a more tolerant (and happier) human being. And we take the opportunity to put our mindfulness practice to the test.

Gratitude is also an antidote to seeing the world as separate from ourselves, and hostile. It's easy to start blaming others or circumstances, and feel as if everything is stacked against us. I used to do that often but it is a no-win place to hang out. It is self-perpetuating. And, it's all in the mind!

Gratitude keeps us grounded and stops the negative spiral from developing, and it's easy to do. It's the low-hanging fruit of mindfulness practice.

So here's a suggestion. This is a core practice and I believe you should try it. Spend a few minutes a day dedicated to listing off all the things you're grateful for. Even better, write them down and read it the next day. Then go off on another round of thank-yous.

You're just an idea experiencing now

Perhaps one of the simplest questions we can ask ourselves is, 'What am I'? To do so is one of the most profound and illuminating practices of all.

First, let's consider our bodies.

First we need to define what is *our* body. The simple place to start would be the skin. Could we say that everything inside the skin is us? Not a bad conclusion, but not so good either. Here's why.

Let's explore the breath. Would you say that once air enters your body it becomes part of you? So the line you would draw is across the nostrils? But what if you open your mouth widely? Is the air in your mouth part of the outside or you? What about the air going down into your lungs? Is that part of you, or just borrowed from the outside? Or maybe the line gets drawn at the lining of the lungs, where the gases interact with the alveoli to allow us to absorb some oxygen atoms.

Are those atoms now 'you'? Take just one. It enters your bloodstream, is processed by your incredible physiology, and helps form a skin cell in your little finger. Now it really is you, Yes?

No! 15 days later that skin cell has had it, gets sloughed off, and the atom of oxygen escapes back to the atmosphere. Did you really own that atom at all, or just borrow it? If you expand this thinking to all parts of your body, where is the self?

In fact, everything that makes up your body is not actually 'you'. Your body is simply a miraculous assembly of borrowed atoms, from air, food and water.

You're 65% oxygen, 18% carbon, 9% hydrogen, 3% nitrogen, plus minerals. You exist and interact continually with the 'outside.' You are simply an event in the wider biosphere. And that's just the human bits!

Up to 90% of the cells in the human body are microbial - we just provide a host environment. Only 10% of you is 'you' to start with.

At the end of the life, what happens to all those molecules? They slowly get recycled and absorbed into something else.

Along the way, from birth to death, we are continually changing and exchanging atoms. All parts get renewed and recycled, sooner or later. So at what point are you exactly 'you'?

In short, we are a dynamic, temporary assembly of atoms, most of which are not human, inside a bag of skin. We cling to an identity. But it is just an idea. And that idea gets us into all kinds of trouble.

Every word we add past 'I am' is simply an idea; our fiction; a set of constructed beliefs. 'I am Simon' means I believe that I am someone called Simon. 'I am a mindfulness teacher' means that I have an idea that this describes me. There's no absolute truth in any of it. The words are just conventions that we use to communicate ideas with others. The truth is, we are just a permeable bag of moving molecules. All we can say with accuracy is 'I am'. All there is for sure is the experience of now. Everything else is fiction.

Kindness and compassion

Matthieu Ricard, a French meditation teacher and monk, was wired up for nueroscientific experiments. The researchers found that when meditating, his high-amplitude gamma synchrony (an indication of happiness) went off the scale, and he has been dubbed the 'happiest man on earth'. When asked what mind state is the happiest, he replied 'compassion'.

Research has shown that we are hardwired to be compassionate, due to what are called mirror neurons. These neurons fire in sympathy with another person so, for instance, if we see someone in pain or distress our own brain is activated in such a way that we recognise the intensity of the other person's experience (ref Tania Singer et al).

Kindness, or compassion, means being with someone in their suffering, without judgement. It means putting our own ego down while we support someone else, even if their problems may be causing unpleasant behaviours. It is a state of selfless attention to others, with altruistic intention.

Like any habit, being kind, or simply wishing others well, may seem clunky at first. Any skill takes practice and as those neural pathways develop it becomes more natural. Kindness and compassion are good habits to develop. Not only is this behaviour likely to benefit others, but there's every chance that you become a nicer person to work with, live with, or do business with, so you'll get on better. Being kind is a win-win situation!

"It is not enough to be compassionate. You must act. There are two aspects to action. One is to overcome the distortions and afflictions of your own mind, that is, in terms of calming and eventually dispelling anger. This is action out of compassion. The other is more social, more public. When something needs to be done in the world to rectify the wrongs, if one is really concerned with benefiting others, one needs to be engaged, involved." The Dalai Lama

Kindness is good business

Kindness is not a word we hear a lot in today's over-busy workplaces. Wellbeing is up there as a concept, but it's a word a bit like sustainability – easy to rattle on about, but highly open to interpretation.

So I wonder if 'kindness' is a simpler, more tangible, and better-understood word to work with. And in my experience, it's a powerful business tool.

Let's take a look at three business phenomena: meetings, conflict, and workload, and see how kindness can be put to work.

But before we dive into the practical applications, let's pause for a moment to explore what goes on in the brain's 85 billion neurons. These cells link up to make sense of the world, connecting along neural pathways. Information from several different parts of the brain - visual, olfactory, aural, and so on, combine with memory to help us identify that a+b =c. That hard cold grey (metal) and soft squidgy (foam) padded thing under my bum is… a chair. So far so good. All our problems, yes all of them, are due to this process of sensory input, recognition, and consequent learned reaction.

However, our brain filters out 99 percent of the information available to us. We *automatically* judge what is important and deserves attention, and discard what is irrelevant. We probably all know someone with a hearing impairment and the frustration they have, as hearing aids amplify all sounds and this filtering does not work so well. We have to do this filtering or there would be too much information to process and we would find it difficult to focus (an interpretation of ADHD).

Intentional focus changes what gets filtered. This is an extremely important concept. *'Having an intention to perform an action increases the activation of its declarative representation in memory'* say *Goschke and Kuhl (1993)*. Put simply this means that if you decide to be kind, opportunities for kindness will appear in your consciousness; they will not get filtered out.

So we can use this in business. Here are three things to try (what have you got to lose?).

1. Meetings. At the start of a good meeting, you will generally set out the length of meeting, agenda etc . Try adding this: 'In this meeting we will be kind to each other'. The communication will change.

2. Conflict. When communication breaks down, or our values and analysis cannot be resolved against someone else's, we can get into conflict. We put up our defences and behave, probably, at our worst. So try this next time. Just think 'kindness' to yourself, and to the other person. It can make a huge difference.

3. Workload. Many, many people feel pressured to do more than they can really cope with (a definition of stress). We can feel bad if we don't get everything done, or done well. So if kindness were a reference point, how would it change things? First we might recognise our good intention to do what we can. We might also have compassion for this human being (ourselves) and do what's possible to relieve some of the pressure. We might negotiate with those making demands, while maintaining the insight that they, too, have pressures and therefore they deserve kindness.

One further suggestion is, at the start of the day, make the commitment that, for example 'today I will be kind whenever I can'. Say it aloud, three times. See what happens. Say it now and see what it feels like.

What motivates us?
- the eight worldly concerns

If we look honestly at what drives us, what motivates us in every action that we take, we will discover that just two forces are at play. The first is wanting, and the second is not wanting. This can be alternatively described as attachment and aversion, or craving and avoidance.

The Buddha identified that wanting or craving, is the source of suffering. We reach towards the things we feel we need, and we reject or avoid the things we fear or which we suspect will create discomfort. We can break these two forces down further, into eight factors in four pairs, which he called *The Eight Worldly Concerns*.

They are as follows:

Material wealth:

a. Seeking money or material wealth, and holding on to them.
b. Fearing losing money or material things.

Praise and blame:

a. Seeking praise and encouragement from others.
b. Fearing getting blamed, ridiculed, or criticised.

Fame or reputation:

a. Seeking the limelight or power.
b. Fearing being ignored or getting a bad reputation.

Sensual experiences:

a. Seeking sensual pleasure or excitement.
b. Avoiding unpleasant experiences, pain or suffering.

If we're successful in getting what we want, we may be delighted, feel warm inside, act with more confidence, and so on. If we're frustrated and don't get what we want, our reaction may be one of anger, anxiety, depression, numbing distraction (you name it!).

You may conclude that simply by devising better strategies to get what you want, and holding on to it tightly, all will be well. It will not. Life is not like that. Sooner or later everything we feel is ours, will slip away, not least our health. And when we die all the wealth in the world is no use to us. Holding on to material wealth, being praised, having a good reputation, and continuing to seek sensual pleasure is not only futile, but it takes a lot of energy and running on that treadmill is a never-ending source of most of our worries and suffering.

The dominant Western paradigm is that being happier means having more. It is incorrect. Whilst that new iPhone may thrill us for a while, we will sooner or later feel it's not enough and crave the next new version when it comes out. If we're stuck in this world view there's no end to dissatisfaction. If we lose our job, or a partner leaves us, or any one of a million random events occur, as they do, will we have the resilience to cope?

It is a very fruitful exercise to explore for ourselves which of the eight concerns is most relevant for us, and how it affects our behaviour. We can use that study to create a new framework by which to live our lives in a way that is meaningful, satisfying, and resilient to life's ups and downs.

Our perception of reality

The world as we experience it, is mostly a construct of our own making.

We take in small amounts of data such as visual information, and create a picture in our heads by adding memory and pattern making, that we then take to be the real thing.

For example, our cone of focused vision is about 5 degrees and outside of this, vision falls increasingly into peripheral vision. Anything in the peripheral zone is unclear, and beyond about 30 degrees is monocular. So in this peripheral zone our brain makes a guess about what the image is, based on past experience.

We 'see' is what's useful, or in evolutionary terms, what's important.

So we think we know what things are, but what we take to be real world objects are mainly created and 'seen' in our mind. We then apply meaning to what we perceive.

We base our understanding of current events on how we assessed similar events previously, so past experience tells us what things mean.

Emotional reactions follow quickly as the amygdala crudely decides if something is good or bad, well before the thinking brain has engaged.

When we're thinking about past events, it's often with a critical reflection on either our own behaviour and activities, or those of someone else. Worst of all, we distort our memories to support our theory of the world.

When we're projecting into the future, we mentally model what will happen based on similar historical events, building pictures and adding the voice-over, making it seem very real. It becomes a self-fulfilling prophecy. Basically, we are continuously rehashing past experience.

So the point is that what we take to be real is mostly of our own invention, and it repeats itself. In this sense, we create the world around us. Whilst we may hope to see things just as they are, I'm not sure that's possible.

What we can do is to recognise the signs of emotions arising in the body in response to our experience, and learn to hold back on our judgements with open-hearted observation.

Mindfulness helps us create a gap between the instinctive reaction and subsequent action. We can then apply well-intentioned choice.

It may also be useful to apply a Zen attitude by telling ourselves that what we see is 'not necessarily so'.

Mind as ocean

If we bring conscious attention to the breathing, we can say to ourselves that as we breathe in, we *know* we are breathing in, and as we breathe out we *know* we are breathing out.

As we settle in, we can start to drop the words and just get the sense and feeling of the knowing. Once this is established, we can extend that knowing to all sense perceptions – of sitting, hearing and so on. There is simply awareness of experience. If the words and concepts are left to dissolve, there is just knowing.

Now setting that observation to one side, let's consider the ocean. What makes up an ocean? Certainly the water, but maybe we can take 'ocean' to mean the whole thing – the water, waves, fishes, dolphins, sea snakes, kelp, and also maybe the sky and weather above the water. All of it is ocean, in different forms.

So when a dolphin jumps clear of the water, we may be delighted and shout 'dolphin jumping', but actually it's just part of the ocean, in temporary form. The dolphin was born in the ocean, was nourished by the ocean, and will dissolve back into the ocean when it dies. It is both of the ocean and one expression of the ocean. However fast it swims, it will never be separate from the ocean. Sharks are no different.

Our minds are an ocean. Our experience, perceptions, thoughts and emotions are like dolphins. They are not separate from mind, they are the form it takes. Mind is the raw material of experience, yet consciousness is formed of experience, so experience is also the raw material of mind.

When we sit in the knowing, we are in and of the ocean.

Mindfulness is the state of attentive non-doing that allows us to float safely and be fully in and of the mind: mind-full-ness.

Holding, adding and letting go

You might like to try a great meditation called 'Mind the Gap'. In whatever you're doing, you simply bring your focus of attention to the gap, for example, between the in-breath and out-breath, between sounds in listening practice, to the blue sky between the clouds, or the moment between one foot placing and the next foot rising.

You simply notice with great refinement, the quality in those gaps. Maybe there's nothing to notice. If that's your experience, you're doing well.

Then you can extend the gap to mean the space around things. This can literally be the space contained by your room for example, rather than the objects in it; the aural environment within which sounds appear, and its relative silence; the sky within which the clouds are passing. Or even the gaps between thoughts (if you're a chatterbox type).

It's good to really spend time with this, until the sense of space and silence and in-between-ness and surrounding-ness becomes really familiar. In a purely scientific sense, solid things are mostly space, at the atomic level.

In fact nothing is solid, nor is it permanent. A 'chair' is the name we give to a certain assembly of wood and materials; but at some point it will break up, so then it's not a chair. Even the darkest rainclouds are really just an expression of temperature, humidity and movement in the atmosphere; so you could say there's really no such thing as a cloud. Or if you insist that there is, you will surely agree that it changes all the time, and at some point will lose its moisture (we know about that phenomenon, in Wales), then dissolve back into the sky; so no one cloud is ever a fixed or independent thing.

The same can be said of 'you', and the 'chair' you're sitting on. So are your thoughts and your identity.

We are not a fixed anything, nor do we have a separate and independent nature. If you were unfortunate enough to be cut cleanly in half, there would be no name imprinted in the cross section like a stick of rock. Not a single cell in your body has your name on it. Who and what you think you are is simply your idea and will die with you.

Every thing that is manifest, is in some way assembled. It has component parts, that by some amazing combination of design, evolution and coincidence has become what it is, starting with the big bang. It is also disassembling as we speak.

You can think of yourself as a river. You are the water, not the river course. So whilst appearances stay roughly the same, or change slowly, the water continually runs on, always changing. From one second to the next, thousands of cells in your body die and get replaced. Your thoughts and emotions change from one moment to the next. If they last longer it is because of something you're doing to prolong them.

So when circumstances arise that make you experience difficult thoughts, feelings and emotions, your reaction and response is something you add on. The circumstance or the thought itself is neutral and transient, and is actually an example of the raw material of everything, which is as insubstantial as a cloud. How you embellish it and believe in it, hold on to it, avoid it or fight it, is stuff you've added. If you don't let it pass on, like the water in the river, that's called clinging.

So in our morning aspiration on retreat we often include the intention to trust in non-clinging awareness. This allows the space to be seen, in and around all things, even the apparently solid ones. It allows things to change as they will, and allows us to observe and let be; to loosen the grip on thoughts and emotions, judgements and opinions.

Or if we notice our tendency to add stuff and hold and react, we make a commitment to let it go, which sooner or later will have an effect, like plugging in a new bit of software.

It's really terribly simple. Just let go, then let go more.

My dear teacher Jangchub, sometimes gives no more instruction on retreat than to say 'relax more'.

String theory

We tie ourselves in knots. To find ways to deal with life's difficulties, we adopt solutions that seem to work, like tying knots in string so that we can grip better. We build ourselves into a complexity of knots and patterns, like some mad and twisted macramé experiment. Our reaction to new problems or threats, is to tighten the knots further or to create new knots. Constantly in fear of unravelling, we pull ever more tightly, create more complex knots, and hold on to these creations with white knuckles.

Yet this does not create happiness. If we want to live more simply and with genuine resilience, we need to let the knots untie. In fact, left alone, the knots will free themselves, with time. We need to let go of the fabrications and the theories we have created to protect ourselves. The knots are concepts, they have no real substance.

Counter-intuitively, the more we let go and the less we protect ourselves, the more secure we are. Fearlessness is about being fully with the experience of whatever arises, without applying our normal analysis of good, bad or ugly.

That requires core strength, which comes from confidence in mind's true nature, which is free of knots. Beneath all our worries and habits of reaction there is freedom and simplicity. True strength is found in this simplicity; this is our true refuge.

So how do we undo the knots, or allow them to do this themselves? It's simply by applying antidotes.

The antidote to suffering is the knowledge that nothing is permanent or just what it seems. So we don't need to make a drama out of a crisis.

The antidote to greed, which feeds self-centredness, is generosity.

The antidote to hatred, which is based on belief of separateness, is connection and compassion.

The antidote to delusion and confusion, is the wisdom that the beneath our worries the mind is pure, clear, loving, empty of predisposition, and that anything is possible.

It's like the sky – despite thunderous rain clouds, the sky itself is clear, blue and spacious. The clouds don't change that.

Jumping to no conclusion

When we are born, almost all is new. We may have already formed some opinions from our womb experience, and have been exposed to the brain chemistry of our mother. But mostly we have to make sense of what we experience, from scratch.

This takes a long time, as we programme our brains to identify shapes and colours, voices, smells and tastes. We also start to categorise things as nice, or as nasty.

The psychologist Oliver Sachs looked closely at people who had experienced brain changes such as stroke, including one individual who suffered a disease creating blindness at birth. In his early twenties this person was given a new laser treatment that suddenly restored his eyesight. But he could not make sense of anything he saw, and never did.

This helps us understand that what we take to be solid and true, is comprised of a small amount of real world information, with a speedy piecing together of old memories, to make sense of it all. 'Oh yes, that's what it is', says our brain.

When faced with something entirely new, we may not even see it at all. Tribes in the Sahara cannot distinguish shades of green, whilst the forms of a complex green picture, like a garden, is strikingly obvious to us from northern Europe.

When it comes to thoughts, feelings and emotions, we give them the same solidity and validity as physical forms. They can 'give' us a bad day, make us angry, give us a warm glow, or cycle around and around with apparently little hope of control. How we react and respond, our likes and dislikes, the things that make us feel good or bad, are just creations of our own learning. This creates our personality.

We can be imprisoned by this patterning, unable to see beyond the walls of our own, constructed, reality. We call the sum of all our patterns 'me', and we think it can't be changed much.

But it can. We don't have to lose everything that makes us to some degree unique, but if we can temper our tendency to jump to a conclusion, with a dose of curiosity and a questioning mind, we may see ways around problems, and be less reactive and judgemental.

In meditation, or anytime when our attention is sharp, we may observe the patterning arising. At this point there can be a temptation to jump on the pattern and swat it down like a fly. Don't. In doing this you give it strength. Just see it, be friendly, and look right through it. It – the thought, feeling or emotion, may have a correlation in real chemistry in the body, but really it is insubstantial. It has no real existence other than that with which we credit it.

As you calmly observe or experience its formation, it will change. It cannot stay the same. By stepping back with attentive observation, it may change quickly.

The more we do this, the less power those old patterns have over us; the less we are pushed around by our karma, the inevitable sequence of causality that follows us like a shadow.

To go further with this practice, ask yourself 'who is the one that is aware of this forming and dissolving'? Or deeper still, notice whether this 'observer' is itself affected by the thought or emotion. Does the 'observer' only appear from time to time, when we bring attention to it, or is it always there? Does the 'observer' have an opinion?

Why you don't want what you want

I was in Portugal last autumn for a retreat. We took a day off to walk by the sea, at a point where the beach had a café and sun loungers. I was struck by an attractive couple settling down for the day. They were wearing the skimpiest of swimsuits, and carrying nothing else apart from the bare essentials – a mobile phone and a selfie stick. Before they were even at their sun loungers, the selfies were being posted to Facebook.

It seems that we are getting drawn into the Facebook world, and dependant for happiness on getting instant likes. I'll not go on about social media, and how research shows it makes us depressed. The point is that this perfectly illustrates the craving mind and the insidious driver of self-referencing.

All day long we're in a constant state of automatically judging what's around us, and whether we want it or don't want it. We build patterns of behaviour around this as a shortcut, so that reactions to familiar stimuli trigger embedded patterns of automated response. We don't even know we're doing this. The philosopher *Alan Watts* said that *'the self is nothing but a pattern of habits.'*

So mindfulness in daily life is actually not about clearing the mind to reach nirvana or an ultimate state of tranquillity. The main point in applied mindfulness, is to be able to take a step back and recognise our patterns of response.

The most insidious and distorting patterns are the ones that are 'about me'. And let's face it, most of what drives us every moment of every day is the judgement about whether something is good or bad for ME.

It's wonderful to see news coverage of disasters. Why: because almost always people are helping each other, in a way that is not self-referencing. They help because compassion naturally drives them to do this. Unfortunately that's rare in daily life, and I'm as guilty as everyone else.

But we should not blame ourselves for this. It's how we've evolved, and it's a helpful way to know if a fruit is good to eat and a tiger is good to run away from. More to the point, is that when we get stressed, our frontal cortex and rational brain gets switched off, so the automation is that much more unfettered.

So how do we get around this and make healthy changes? Simply by being aware of present moment feelings.

I've just seen some research into using mindfulness for addiction (Elwafi et al 2013). They asked smokers to really tune-in to the taste and body feeling of smoking. Some found for the first time that they didn't actually like it. The pattern of reaching for a cigarette when 'needed' was broken, just like that, and continued practice led to good rates of giving up smoking.

So all that was needed was this tuning-in. Try it now as you read this. Stop thinking, start feeling. If you need help, bring attention to whatever physical sensation is in your right foot now; as you do this, be aware that you are in the present moment – you cannot do it otherwise.

So here's a three-part mindfulness practice in a nutshell: pay attention, relax, and be curious.

Now, of course we do all this mindfulness is because what we really want is peace, calm, and great insights. Yes? Go get them! Oops, have I just set up another craving? Beware of this pitfall and of the paradox, that if you put off happiness to another time and another set of conditions, you will not reach it. If you go hunting for something, it will elude you. Let it come to you.

You might find deep contentment in an Ashram, in the pub, or under the sofa, but actually you don't need to go anywhere. It's available right here, now.

The non-stick mind

I love to cook eggs (the trick with fried eggs is to cook them on a really slow heat, with butter, with a lid). But even the newest frying pan can still stick a bit.

We suffer emotionally for one reason only; that stuff the world throws at us, we take personally. It sticks, and we contort ourselves to shake it off, or to try to avoid it in the first place. How would it be if any insult, any loss, any embarrassment, or any pain, was clearly experienced, but our emotional reaction to it simply did not hang around for long?

Well, the good news is that our innate mind, the one we were born with, is entirely non-stick. In fact, there's nothing there for anything to stick to.

So if that's true for all of us (which it is), how come we're screwed up by life? Why is it that we worry about stuff that's happened, might happen, or might not happen? What causes the stickiness? And what can we do about it?

My personal experience, as one who is not yet fully Teflon-coated (but working at it), is that the problem is me. Yeah, that Simon fellow with all his habituated ways and distorted perceptions. I can only experience the non-stick quality, the non-material spaciousness of the innate mind, when I've dropped the concept of me. All the stickiness, is stuff that sticks to Simon.

So it seems as if the simple solution is to let go of our learned reactions and behaviours. If only it was really that simple, right? Ok, maybe we get glimpses on the cushion, but how can we bring that freshness and resilience into daily life?

Again, I can only talk from my own experience; and the news that you don't want to hear is that progress comes from regular sitting practice and retreats – just being there, patiently, until insights turn up. More and more glimpses of the truth of the bare, naked mind; more and more confidence in this; and more likelihood that this truth starts to permeate everyday life, so that emotional reactions begin to shorten and lessen in intensity. I don't think there's a short cut.

And what do you do when you're sitting? Absolutely nothing; just stay awake! Less and less effort is the answer. When you stop making any effort at all, not even the slightest effort, you are truly letting go. You must even let go of letting go. And if you let go completely, what can stick?

So this is really the practice I want to share with you. You can call it mindfulness if you wish, or dharma, or something more spiritual. They're just words. What's clear to me is that this is the most beautiful thing there is; so that's worth sharing. That, and good ways to cook eggs.

I think, therefore I'm not

Descartes was wrong when he said 'I think, therefore I am' (IMHO). Thinking is probably the biggest smokescreen to getting insight into what we really are. It's the #1 problem in meditation.

Right now, to stay with the experience of this moment, no thought is required. If we're aiming to 'be in the present moment', it actually requires us to step back from thoughts.

It's like being at the centre of a wheel. The further out you go the faster you spin, but right at the very, very centre there's a place where there's no movement at all. You can spin your thoughts further and further away from this moment and get dizzily lost in the past or future, or you can come closer and closer to the still centre of now, where there are no thoughts at all.

Ok, so now I hear you ask, can I be in the moment and still be thinking, which might be a positive and creative or otherwise useful thing to do? Yes, you can, but it takes skill and familiarity with present moment awareness (through practice!). It's too easy to get carried away in analysis or fantasy, and then find that the day has gone by and that we've never really been alive and present at all – a day of not living *in* the present moment. That doesn't mean we should live *for* the moment, as that implies hedonism. Our aim is to live fully, *and* to plan skilfully, with wholesome motivation.

You may also be wondering how to 'get rid' of thoughts. There you are, being good and sitting on the cushion, when ten million thoughts pop up, enjoying the limelight.

Ok, so experience the fact that thoughts arise, and that they dissolve again. In fact if you bring your attention to the fact that there's thinking; you just say 'thinking'. As soon as you catch yourself thinking, just say 'thinking'. And be friendly to those naughty thoughts! Just smile at them.

Sooner or later, if you're paying attention, you'll see a gap between thoughts. Wonderful – the sequence of thoughts has now become your opportunity for deep practice. Or you may realise that the thought itself is not separate from your mind, so it illustrates the infinite possibility of mind.

The other factor is that we're always 'doing' something, even if we're not thinking about it. We are masters in keeping busy or distracted. If you're looking for a full-on experience of Now, you have to Stop. Doing. Anything.

So the instruction, if you want one, is to 'rest in the continuity of now'. That means allowing thoughts to arise if they will, but not engaging. No pushing way, no seeking, no meditating. Don't even try to do nothing. Just rest, with alertness. If you hit the sweet spot, even for an instant, where there is no resistance or wanting, bliss arises.

You may also reflect later, that in that sweet moment, you were not there. There's awareness, but no 'me'. To some people this can be scary, but I assure you that it's totally safe. It's actually our true nature.

How to rest the mind

We all know how to rest our bodies, right? Just put your feet up, slouch, and do nothing. Simple. But how do you rest the mind?

What we need to cultivate is the part of the brain that appears to be much more random or pixelated than the more linear, verbal part we are more familiar with. We get in touch with this part of the brain in the arts, music, sport and whenever verbalisation is not required.

Resting the mind is a bit like going to sleep, only you stay awake! The one trick is to be 100% present. If you can just let data from your senses flow through without any data processing (comments or judgements) then stay in this flow of now-ness, you can rest the body and the mind. It's a state of being awake yet totally restful.

So how do we do this?

As soon as you notice a sentence starting to form, just let it dissolve; don't finish the sentence. The other thing to watch for is images forming. As soon as you notice a picture appearing in your mind, actively let it dissolve.

Consider what happens when we go to sleep. To nod off, we have to relax, trust our body to take care of us and to let go of the normal pattern of logical thinking.

You may we need a prop to support you in this process of noticing words or images arising. This brings us back to experiencing the breath. Given that the breath is always moving, following its progress without distraction helps you stay present. Once you experience this now-ness with bare attention, you will see that it's a place of great spaciousness and freedom. And that's a good place to rest and a great way to go to sleep.

Then in the morning, try to catch the first moment of waking, and with the first in-breath, drop into pure attention then as well. It can be a moment of amazing clarity.

Every step takes us closer

Mindful walking is one of the simple but profound joys of mindfulness practice. When walking mindfully, you're on the path! So here's how to do it.

I'm guessing that at some point in your day you'll walk somewhere. If that's outside, so much the better. So you have a great opportunity for mindfulness practice. No excuses. Even a walk down the corridor to the loo is a perfect opportunity to practice. All those short walks may add up to a good bit of mindfulness practice every day.

There are just three things to remember. Interest, kindness, and connection. I'll explain.

Interest: Most of the time we walk around in a zombie state. We only notice what we've are in the habit of noticing. Ninety-nine percent of potential stimuli, especially visual, never gets into our consciousness. The brain does this filtering because if it didn't the world would be overwhelming. People with ADHD notice everything; every bug, every piece of glitter, every touch of a breeze, every word on a T-shirt 100m away. That's not useful, because they get distracted all the time. Somewhere in the middle is mindful attention.

This means opening up our attention, and the key tool to that is interest. If we make a deliberate effort to notice more of what's around us, it's nearly always rewarding. Suddenly you may hear a bird singing, see the play of light on the leaves of a tree, or notice a passing smile from a complete stranger.

Or you could take more interest in your own experience. How your body moves, joint by joint and muscle by muscle; how perspective changes as you move through space and how; how particular smells quickly trigger emotional reactions or memories how sounds come and go without leaving any trace.

So just open up the senses, and take a deep interest in what you experience.

Kindness: The second factor in mindful walking practice is to be kind. While doing all that noticing, you'll probably also see more suffering. You'll notice that someone you're passing is frowning, a bit stooped, or involved in an aggressive phone call. You may see the masks we all wear to protect ourselves, whether that's being cool, submissive, or uber-confident.

There's a huge need for kindness, to ourselves as well as to others. Now, if you want the deepest, most secret teaching on this, I'll give it to you. If you're not ready just stop reading immediately… ok, so you're ready?

Smile. That's it. Smile more.

Smile at total strangers (by the way most will smile back– I've never had anyone hit me yet). Smile at your colleagues. Smile at the paving slabs and slugs. It doesn't have to be a big cheesy smile. In fact it may be imperceptible, but inside, you're smiling. With everything you see, and hear, and smell, just wish it well. Not just pretty things; all things.

Connection: We live as if we lead separate lives and have control. Connection is the third key. We can breathe only because trees give off oxygen. We have energy because the sun hit a leaf, somewhere on a farm, and some poorly paid worker harvested the crops that got processed by someone else and ended up in our cereal bowl. We've got a job because someone thought up the idea of the business, that didn't exist before. We're about as independent as a molecule of water in a river.

We are totally supported by all that's around us, and if we ever stopped to think about it we might even be grateful, instead of taking it all for granted.

More pointedly, if we're looking for good reasons to be a bit more aware of this, there's the principle of karma; the idea that your actions will come around and affect you later. Don't we all love it when the baddy gets what he deserves? Behave like a spoilt child and you'll probably see a negative effect quite soon. Take all that supports you for granted and you might find that some things stop flowing.

So, while you walking with interest and kindness, be thankful for all the connections that support you. Don't just wish peace for yourself, but for everyone and everything.

The path of mindfulness, is here, in front of us, right now. There's nowhere else you can be, so make the most of it. When you do that, every step, ever so slightly, generates more peace in the world.

Fear, trust and refuge

When we embark on the exploration that is mindfulness, we make a journey into the unknown. To develop insights into the nature of mind we need to be open to whatever the mind reveals to us, and to begin with accepting that we don't know what this will be. So there is, inherent in this process of exploration, uncertainty and a certain level of fear.

It's like setting sail in a boat that has no rudder and no charts. To get into the boat you have to have trust that it will lead somewhere useful. But if you stay on the shore, you will go nowhere.

For this reason, the traditional starting point in Buddhist meditation is to 'take refuge'. In effect this means having trust in the practice. To begin with one puts that trust in 'buddha nature' (our in-built, pure, compassionate mind). Next one puts trust in these ancient teaching practices then, finally, in the community of other people who support us on this journey.

We can let go more easefully into the unknown realm of our mind, by just having confidence that these simple practices have worked for millennia to help ordinary people cope better with life, and to experience joy in the miracle of being alive and conscious. If you're on this journey, and guided by someone who knows the ropes and abides the traditional teaching model (however creatively presented!) you will be ok.

That's not to say that it's all blissful and exciting. In our meditation practice, just as in life, we can experience boredom, irritation, dullness, anger and doubt. In fact that exact sequence is very commonly experienced, perhaps several times in each meditation session. You may get stuck on one of them, or you may cycle through them again and again. Watch for this and be aware that it's quite normal.

Meditation can be blissful, it can be dull, and it can be downright unpleasant. The starting point is stepping back to observe and feel what goes on in the body (most emotions are just bodily sensations). Just be curious, accepting and interested.

To explore what we are fearful of we need to look at ego or identity. Who we think we are (and consequently our views) become very fixed, influencing all of our thoughts and actions. We're very quick to respond if something challenges us – making a judgement that we dislike something, or like it, then acting on those impressions without stopping to question their truth and our habitual ways.

We hold this self-image and these views very tightly and protect them. In meditation, we're in a process of loosening the grip. At some stage we may let it fall away entirely, and just experience life as it happens directly and without judgement (which is blissful). But as soon as the ego notices that it has been made redundant, it jumps up like a child with a tantrum. At that point one of the distractions will arise. For example – 'this is so boring', or 'this is a load of rubbish' or 'I'm no good at this'.

There is a clear correlation between advances in the practice, and letting go of our self–referencing. The bigger the letting-go, eventually to the point of freefall, the bigger the potential for insight becomes. The art of mindfulness is to stay awake, in the here and now, while experiencing this freefall. Refuge helps you do this.

My root teacher, Namgyal Rinpoche, described enlightenment as 'having one foot over the abyss and one on solid ground'.

So I invite you to step into that rudderless boat, with me and every other explorer into the nature of the mind. Let your heart be your navigator, and let the wisdom that you seek be the wind in your sails. Just let go. All will be fine.

Go ahead and die a bit

Let's get right down to basics. There are two drivers in our lives; love and fear. They come in many shapes and sizes. Which is dominant for you?

Love of course, I hear you say. You're trying to do the right thing and be the best person you can, right?

If so, why is it that we get negative emotional reactions? Why do we lash out when threatened or insulted? Or run away, or make a joke, or pretend it never happened.

In essence we have two responses to something new. We like it, or we don't. Occasionally things are neutral.

With stuff we like, we want it, and more of it. We miss it if we don't get it.

With stuff we don't like, we get very inventive at avoiding it. If we can't avoid it, we might get depressed, or feel helpless.

Push and pull, all day long. Most of it is so built–in to our behaviours that we don't even notice it happening. Others might see what we do, and if their reaction is a different one, they may think we're odd, or judge us negatively. (Not that we'd do that to them, right?)

Well, all that push and pull actually comes from fear. We've amassed a shed load of evidence that has helped shape a fictional character we have called 'me'. All our life experience and cultural conditioning has honed this character, and each time we respond according to our learned patterns, the patterning gets stronger. This is the ego.

Ego is touchy and always on guard, ready to fend off attack. This is why meditation can be a challenge. In meditation, we get under the ego's radar. The ego doesn't like the loss of control. The predominant driver of ego is fear.

So what would happen if, even just for one second, we dropped the whole thing? In a sense this is about letting ourselves die for a bit; not our bodies, which have systems for keeping the organism alive; but the fictional edifice known as 'me' which normally runs the show. Or thinks it does.

So if we let the whole thing disassemble and drop, what would be left?

I was very moved by an event in the last Olympics. Two brothers were winning a long distance race, when the leader suddenly, 50m from the finish line, totally lost the plot from sheer exhaustion. He had no sense of forwards or backwards. His brother, a few metres behind, immediately went to his rescue, propped him up as he stumbled on, and threw him over the line, losing his own medal in the process.

That was not ego-driven. It was pure compassion. Love.

When we drop the ego, a higher intelligence takes over. When a musician or artist is in the flow of his work, there is no ego. When a coach is there entirely for the client, his ego is not in the room. When we know something is right, rather than figure it out, ego does not come into it.

So how do you practise this? Let me emphasise that first there must be deep tranquillity. Don't try it otherwise. This is an advanced practice. If you know how to get a to a point of real stillness and tranquillity, and when you know you're ready, just let go. Let go of everything. Every concept, every memory, every single one of the billion little events which have led to this moment. It takes a couple of seconds. Then you can come back to where you were. But just maybe, for an instant, you will have experienced a freshness, a moment when there was complete freedom.

What's the problem with Ego?

At some point in our mindfulness practice, we will have the insight that how we think and act are just habits. More fundamentally, we realise that we are not our thoughts. If that's so, who's in control? And who's noticing the thoughts?

A lot of mindfulness practice can be seen as a process of letting go of fixed views, and opening up the mind to other possibilities. We start to realise that we've created a monster called Ego, and we want to be the hero and slay it and then we'll be fine and everyone will be amazed at our equanimity. This approach is flawed.

First of all, it's true that we are ego-driven. Ego is our self-image, our identity. Above all it is a belief that we are separate and must protect ourselves from all that is not us. We've carefully assembled our identity like a unique house, adding an extension here, a new coat of paint there, reinforcing the foundations, and - in particular - making it weather-proof and burglar-proof.

It's been a lifelong project so any threat to this, to who we believe we are, including our opinions or our possessions, must be dealt with swiftly and effectively. If our evasion or aggression preserves the edifice it just shows what a great, resilient structure it is. Good job. Hold on to it even tighter.

The problem is that it's not just a house. It's also a prison. We put so much energy into holding it together that we miss out on the possibility of life's adventure. We fail to see beyond our limited view. We might even put a sign on the door saying 'keep out'.

But inevitably, sooner or later, the roof will leak and the walls will crumble. We get ill, everything goes pear-shaped, we die. Shit happens. The only thing we can be sure of is change. And much of it will be beyond our control. To be okay with uncertainty is to survive and grow, to swim with the tide, or even to surf the waves.

Our Ego is not an enemy.He's a loyal bodyguard, keeping a watchful eye out for threats. He's just a bit too touchy and over-protective at times.

Rather than battling to get rid of our Ego, it is more helpful to get to know him, and to thank him for his constant attention, but to give him time off. For it is only when we allow our fears and demons to be present, yet be unmoved by them, that we can open up to new experiences and see the world with fresh eyes.

The joy of being a nobody

I have just walked home after dropping my daughter to school. As I walked through town and then the park, it struck me how unhappy most people looked. Some were looking stressed, some vacant, but most of all it just seemed that everyone was making a huge effort to be 'a somebody' ... and probably failing to meet their own ideal self-image.

Being *somebody* takes energy. It's an internal battle. It means dressing in a particular way, communicating in a particular way, having our own particular thoughts cycling around in our head. It also means using vast reserves of energy maintaining this outward and inward identity all day long.

It struck me in particular when I passed by a group of about 30 French students. Of course what they all had in common was that they were French and they were visiting Cardiff. Whilst each was conforming to a dress code and trying to fit in, each one of them also made sure that they maintained their individuality, whether it was in the way they walked, the way they looked at each other with a smile or frown, the particular choice of clothes and hair style.

This then led me to start thinking about anthills! Anyone who's watched a David Attenborough programme will have seen how communities of animals such as ants are, in effect, one large organism. By some miracle of chemical signalling, (a kind of anternet!) they find a common purpose and each individual knows what to do in contributing to the needs of the community.

How would it be if we humans dropped every concept of 'me'?

This is quite easy to try out. Next time you take a walk, whether that's down the street or through the office, try, if only for a minute, to drop all concepts and memories of who you are.

Just for a minute, be a *nobody*.

For that short while, try to cultivate the sense that every human you see is just like you, and part of one, multi-particled human organism.

My experience of this exercise is that it quite naturally cultivates a sense of empathy and kindness.

How would it be if there were a bit more of a sense of inter-dependence, a bit more cultivation of compassion, and a bit less of individuality and self-obsession; a bit more trust and a bit less fear; a bit more peace and a bit less war?

And it can start only here, with us.

Maps, view and intention

When I began to learn nautical navigation, it struck me how different sailing charts were to the Ordnance Survey maps I was used to reading. The land element of charts is simplified, showing only what matters to the sailor: high points and landmarks; harbours, and navigational points for alignment and so on. From the other perspective, land maps show almost nothing about the sea. They omit underwater contours, obstructions, and information about currents because, on land, you don't need to know these things.

We can make only an approximate model of the reality around us, through the tools of our senses and previous experience.

The nature and limitations of our mental maps determine the nature and limitations of our interpretation of reality and our response to it. Unfortunately we may not get the map right, like those distorted medieval maps with ships falling off the edge of the world based on the cartographer's view of reality.

Maps are not the territory. If we have a different map, we will experience life differently. The happy fact is that we are all cartographers. We can revise our own map should we find flaws in it. Or better still, we may even touch on a way of looking at the world which allows us to experience things without pre-judgement, just as they are, right now, as if seen for the first time. Even to have no map.

When this happens we are more able to savour reality as it is, without the judgements reflected in the map we have created for ourselves. This process of recognition is called *insight*. We start to see how our experience of reality is programmed by our own learned patterns – our map.

With patience and self-compassion, we can accept our shortcomings and recognise the pattern-making. With no more than simple acceptance, the patterns and the map can begin to change. The only tool we need is to tune in to our innate awareness, which is patiently operating all the time, offering us all the wisdom we ever need.

How the map changes depends on our *view* and *intention*.

If we go bird spotting, for instance, we will see lots of birds that we would normally miss, because our attention is open and we're looking for birds.

If our intention is to help others, we will notice opportunities to do this too.

The theory of relativity

I worry about driverless cars. This technology, involving sat navs and other GPS devices relies critically on the Theory of Relativity to work. In a nutshell, movement in space and time can only be measured in relation to other objects.

We're like this too: we judge our position, movement and progress in this world, physically as well as emotionally, in relation to other people, objects, and time. Our identity, who and what we think we are, and our view of success or failure have meaning only in relation to other people and things. How much stuff we have, like money and material possessions, how well we're getting on in our relationships at work and home, how attractive we think we are, how quickly we achieve something, or how stuck we seem, are all about the relationship between 'me' and 'not me'; me and other. This is called *duality*.

Imagine for a moment what it would be like to let go of this tangible sense of self and all the worries it brings. What would it be like to get behind the mask and inhabit the consciousness that watches this human play unfolding in all its angst and joys. This bare consciousness does not measure itself against 'other' because it has no form or identity.

When you hit this bedrock of reality in meditation, it's no surprise that you can sit for ages without getting uncomfortable or bored. There is no sense that this is 'my' body as a separate thing. It is no more special or interesting (or *just as* special and interesting) as the sound of the bird outside the window or the wind blowing. In the place of all the normal me-centred evaluation is simply interest and joy in the ever-changing nature of things.

So now back to daily life! If even a smidgeon of this truth gets into our heads, it will start to affect our relationships with the people and things we encounter. We will start to allow the present to be as it is, because we no longer need to defend the Self against everything else. We will allow the change to happen because we are powerless to do otherwise.

Insults and losses will hurt less. You will love more, with less conditionality. There will be more joy, because you will see things more for what they are rather than for their impact on to you.

Awareness: there's nothing to it

Mindfulness is a wonderful practice, which can be dressed up in all kinds of techniques and measured by neurological science. But if we really hone it down, there's just one insight that matters. Without it, the practice is groundless and ineffective.

This insight is the heart of the teaching.

Let's take sound as an example. We can tune-in mindfully to the sounds around us at any time. This, in itself, is a great practice that opens our mind to our environment.

But there's a fascinating twist in mindful listening. As you listen, bring your attention not to the sounds, but to the 'space' in which the sounds arise; the gaps between the sounds; the air through which the sound waves travel.

Another example of mindful awareness could be with your body. As you read this, do a quick scan and find any part of your body that is a little uncomfortable, or better still, wait for an itch. Don't move. Be aware of the discomfort. Notice how it clammers for your attention, and then, purposefully widen your attention beyond the discomfort or itch. Realise that awareness is much bigger than the thing we bring our focus to.

Underneath, or behind, or around, or within all sense perception, there is just naked awareness; awareness without comment; with no preferences (too loud / too buzzy, too achy/ too itchy). It's always available. It's the space in which the sounds we hear appear. It's the baseline awareness in which body sensations appear. It's also the field of mind in which thoughts appear.

Everything else–the sounds, the itches, the thoughts–are like waves splashing around taking up most of our attention. Get under the surface, or bring to mind the whole ocean. All these sounds and itches and thoughts and waves are temporary appearances. The ground of awareness is always there, and always unaffected by events.

So we have this contradiction: awareness is the raw material of everything we perceive; yet of itself, it has no form, no predisposition, and no comment. It's just a field of infinite possibility. Knowing this creates freedom, and the opportunity for change.

What if we stopped dreaming?

We know from neuroscience that what we experience is largely our own creation. We take very small amounts of highly selected real world data from our senses (mainly sight), add in a large measure of memory, do some crude pattern recognition, and make a movie in our minds. Then we take this to be the real thing.

I have learned a lot from my lovely daughter, who has ADHD. She notices everything. There is almost no filter of 'unnecessary' data. So yesterday morning we went for an early walk in the park, and on the way back we were headed to the bakery for a croissant. My attention was on the shop window and my focus was on bakery products. My daughter spotted a person we know in a passing van in the busy road. I would never in a million years have noticed her. If I'd been alone the friend would not, in my reality, have been there.

Later that day, I was looking at an article about the rain forest. I have seen tropical vegetation, but my real image of the rainforest comes from television and glossy magazines. Using those sources of inspiration, I can shut my eyes and walk through a rainforest in my head.

We do this when we are dreaming. We all know dreams can be very real, colourful and potent, if a little weird at times. But dreams show us how creative the mind can be. It only needs a spoonful of real world data to make the difference between waking and dreaming. It's an important distinction. We could ask ourselves how much stress in daily life, with all its little sufferings, is caused by our dream-like creations.

What would happen if we could drop all the dreaming? If we could let go of everything we've ever known, of all the memories and preferences and opinions that make up 'me'? What if we could experience even one moment with fresh eyes, fresh ears, fresh nose and mouth, fresh sensations and an open mind?

If you try this, in your formal meditation practice, you may hit fear. It's far from easy to drop all our preconceptions, especially about who we are, and it requires huge stability, tranquillity, trust and bravery. It takes practice.

We hold on to all these views and assumptions because letting go of it is about letting go of the 'me' we think we are. It can feel like dying or stepping into the abyss. But actually, it's fine. Step into the abyss and there you will find the pervading love, gently holding you. No fuss. In fact it's very, very funny once you realise that it's always been there. And very awful, because you see how people suffer unnecessarily.

To summarise, we stress out over events yet we are the main creator of our reality. We interpret and create near-dream experience all the time and put great effort into constructing and defending the mirage of who we are.

But my main message to you is one of encouragement, to let you know that by letting go more, by relaxing more into fresh attentiveness, we can discover the world is far more supportive than threatening; and that life holds us dearly.

Timelessness and stillness

Let's contemplate the nature of time.

I sometimes ask people in my classes, 'in which direction does time travel?' It's a kind of Zen riddle, as it challenges the mind. Of course the answer is that there is no answer.

If we think of the flow of events as a river, time can be seen as the flowing water. This is normally the way we think of it. Alternatively, we can consider that time is the riverbed, past which events move. This latter analogy is the one I find interesting.

In this scenario, time does not move, but is the still point past which events move and change. If we now leave the river analogy, time can be seen as a neutral unchanging viewpoint, from which awareness witnesses the ever-changing arising and dissolving of moments of manifestation.

You can bring this into meditation. You become the witness, the still point from which anything that arises and changes, or dissolves, is viewed. The arising can be your breathing, a plane flying past, or the sound the fridge makes. You don't need to get involved, you're just a neutral observer, without comment or judgement, unaffected by all that arises and dissolves.

This is the state of pure mindfulness.

By the way, the arising and dissolving can also mean things moving because, for example, if you take a snapshot of a moving train then another one second later, it will have moved of course, and all the people inside it will have moved as well. From a moment-to-moment perspective it is a new assemblage in space/time of its component atoms. However brief those moments are cut, even if infinitely small, it's always subtly changing. Nothing stays the same, ever.

Now, let's take the meditation a step further. Can you take 'you' out of the equation and just witness awareness experiencing all this ever-changing manifestation? Rest there. If it gets a bit scary step back to you, come back to observing your breath for a moment, then drop in again. Short moments of insight are better than holding on for dear life.

Enjoy the meditations. Then when you're back at work with an irritating colleague or dealing with the builder who has just messed up your new bathroom, see if something of this non-reactiveness can be useful. It may give you a moment to step back and be a bit less judgmental; which makes everyone's day a little better.

Where did the time go?

Let's go back to our day-to-day concept of time. It progresses, and its indicator is change. We see things that have already happened as the past, and things we can imagine happening as the future. Somewhere in the middle is now, though exactly where is elusive.

This is a bit like space. The earth is, apparently, hurtling through space, and also spinning. We don't experience this, unless we look at the sun's path across the sky and observe the stars moving above us. So this movement can only really experienced in relation to another object in the universe.

When our meditation allows us glimpses of the transcendental, one insight is that there is no time there. This timeless and formless source of awareness is called Sunyata, the Tao, the raw energy of life, or 'Emptiness'. But the term 'Emptiness' can often be a confusing description because, despite the absence of form, colour, and so on, this empty space has infinite possibilities to shape itself into all phenomena.

The Buddha explained this by saying that phenomena are empty of distinct and unique identity. All phenomena are assembled from elemental components, are dependent for their assembly on conditions, and are temporary. In this way they are empty of *independent identity*. This empty field of endless possibilities is like an ocean. We're not talking about molecules of water or the waves or the fish; we're talking about the whole concept of 'ocean'.

Another aspect to this no-thing is that because it does not change in its essence, it therefore has no past or future. It was not created and it will not cease. It has no time.

So that's the conundrum. In our daily lives we see change and watch the clock, yet in our deepest knowing we understand that time is not like that. Time can sometimes appear to speed up or drag on, or even be quite still, depending on what we're doing and our state of mind. This may be truer than we allow it to be within the conceptual confines of 'clock time'.

I don't have an answer to this. It just makes life more interesting and full of wonder. The more we have reason to question the model we're in, the more likely we are to find it fun to be here, with a sense of freedom from our normal confines. And when we do, we wonder where the time went.

A terrible accident…

Imagine that you have been involved in a terrible accident. Despite all their best efforts, the medical team have had to amputate your left arm. They patch you up and you leave the hospital.

Two days later you're distracted by looking at a crane as you cross the street. A builder's truck comes round the corner at a crazy speed at that very moment, knocking into your right shoulder. You end up in hospital again, and despite all their considerable efforts, the surgeons have to amputate your right arm.

This takes some adjustment. Nevertheless you recover and go about life in this new way. Then, a few weeks later, there is … a terrible accident! Unbelievably, both your legs have been crushed. Despite hours in surgery, the only solution is to amputate both legs.

After some recovery time, you're allowed out of the hospital. Your friend pushes your wheelchair, but he's not quite with it today as his wife has just run off with the BMW. So in his distraction, he lets go of the wheelchair on a slope down towards the main road. The resulting accident is appalling. Hours of surgery lead to only one option: to remove the body and keep your head on a life support system. This actually works pretty well.

All seems fine, but you do seem to be having a bad run of luck, and one day, when leaning over to pick up a pen in your teeth, your head rolls away and into the organic waste bin. By the time someone realises the mistake, your head has been macerated and is being composted. All that's left intact is one small piece of flesh. They rush this to the new trauma unit in the hospital, and by a miracle of engineering and bionics, restore you to a functional life so that you can go back to work.

Just when all seems fine, there's a terrible gas leak in the office and everything in it gets vaporised.

But, from just one cell captured from the fallout, they manage to rebuild your whole body with bionic parts. But your brain, of course, has long gone and with it all your memories, opinions, and cultural preferences.

Now, ask yourself this question:

Where, and what, are 'you'?

1000 moments to a mindful life

In his book *Outliers: The Story of Success,* Malcolm Gladwell (who also wrote The Tipping Point) makes a convincing case for the "10,000-Hour Rule", claiming that the key to achieving real mastery in any skill is about practising for a total of around 10,000 hours. For the nerds amongst you, that's 6 years of working 7 hours each working day.

So how long does it take to master mindfulness?

Well, the answer is anything between about 10 seconds and 20 years.

Why the disparity? It can be 10 seconds, because that's about how long it takes to take three mindful breaths. If you can do that perfectly (I'll explain at the end of the book) you may 'get it' right away.

On the other hand if, like most of us, you need to work at it and do, say, one hour of mindfulness each day plus, say, two weeks on retreat, that adds up to twenty years. It took me fifteen years to understand the nature of mind – in a three second insight on retreat at 10.15 am on July 1st 2013. It was the pivotal moment in my life. Because of that moment, my life is now dedicated to helping others to 'get it', but more quickly!

So, I'm guessing that you're looking for the shortcut! Okay, here are the conditions that must be met in your three mindful breaths:

- Attention – for example by staying focused on the physical sensations on the breath

- Tranquillity – feeling settled, relaxed and grounded with no niggling
- Curiosity – being interested, without self-referencing
- Patience – opening a gap in time/space with no past or future referencing
- Not wanting – not wanting anything to change, just allowing the present to roll out
- Compassion – being committed to the exploration of your own mind, so that you can help others better

Ok so off you go! It's easy. Simply be present.

Ah, so you just tried it and it didn't work? Maybe your mind went AWOL? Maybe a few more hours are needed. Maybe you need some guidance.

That's why, in my training work with organisations, I base the courses on very short exercises, practised often. The most important are the ten-second exercises to tune-in and re-boot. If you can do one an hour, for two months, that's one thousand mindful moments.

Keep that up, and you're going to change your life for the better, for sure. Moment by moment you will be edging towards those 10,000 hours, and opening up the possibility for deeper insight.

Don't fight with the present – really?

'Don't fight with the present', we hear people say. Mostly I'm wary of one-liners and memes. I think most people use them to sound cool and wise. But I often wonder whether the person uttering the one-liner fully understands what they mean.

'Don't fight with the present', however, happens to be profound. I'll explain why.

It comes down to suffering... Oh no, you may think, here goes another Buddhist banging on again. Call it what you like, understanding suffering is at the heart of awakening.

We spend pretty much every waking moment in states of clinging or avoidance and governed by fear.

We cling to ideas about who we are and who we want to become; about the fall of our hair and the way we speak and what we have to say, so that we look good; about the position we're sitting or standing in because that communicates something too; and ideas about the role we play to earn a living–as if being lawyer / father / nurse / teacher / coach explains everything about us.

Or maybe we hold on for dear life to the digitised numbers in a bank account we call our money; to the tin box we call our car; to the cotton in the clothes we wear; or the bricks and mortar we call home. We fear their loss, and we strive for gain.

We avoid discomfort by crossing or uncrossing our legs; shifting a little; unbuttoning something or putting on a jumper; by not reading something unpleasant–or reading it again and again as if it might change; by not confronting someone who has just, however mildly, put us down or been insensitive; or by putting off the difficult task that's hovering.

Or maybe we avoid unpleasant feelings with time on Facebook, or looking out the window, or making yet another cuppa, by watching crap on the TV, or gossiping. We can find one of a million ways to not be present, in case a demon jumps in to the space we might create and eats us up.

So when we feel discomfort of the kind we can't name, the itchy need for Something Else – we then seek a fix, like needing another coffee or a melted cheese panini, or fantasising about the girl/boy in the corner of the coffee shop, or the better job we deserve, or the accolade we hope for. We need to change something, fiddle the dials.

What is all this? What's the common factor? It's suffering! As humans, we suffer. Not just the big stuff, like dying or divorce or being made redundant, but tiny, mostly un-noticed stuff. All day, every moment, the desire for something other than what is present, now, creates suffering.

It takes up our energy and attention and, in doing so, hinders our capacity to see opportunities, to tune in emotionally to other people, or simply to enjoy the richness around us. This yearning stops us living fully.

To acknowledge and accept all this discomfort, with curiosity, is at the heart of meditation practice. Acceptance does not mean submission. It is right that we work towards things getting better. But *right now* is the only time we have to live, so we better stop fussing. And that means being open and fearless to *what is,* now. After all, most of our discomfort is immaterial, comprising passing thoughts and sensations.

When we're open and friends with the present in this way, we get to know the truth of the insubstantial, self-created and temporary nature of most of this discomfort. In seeing it for what it is, it doesn't hang around. And in the gaps of present moment attention that then get created, we get to experience the open, spacious nature of the ground of Being, and its infinite possibilities.

This is 'full catastrophe living', to quote John Kabat-Zinn quoting Zorba. Fight the present and you will never win. Cherish it and you will start to awaken, moment by moment.

Facing-off fear

I've come to realise that, for me, the only thing that holds me back is fear. When I feel fearless, I am powerful, and flourish. Nothing can stop me achieving anything (or at least giving it a go).

Our instinctive pattern is to protect ourselves from harm and, when it comes to emotional disturbance, we protect ourselves in complex ways.

Emotional pain comes in many forms. It may be a sudden tsunami of reaction to a disturbing event or it can be a mild, but persistent, undertow from an on-going issue that drags us down. And by the way, emotions are basically experienced as body sensations.

What do we do when these triggers arise, whether they be external or even from our own thoughts?

In essence there are two reactions: fight or flight. The fight reactions are more obvious, with aggression, blame and bubbling anger toward self or others. But the ones to watch for are the flight reactions such as distraction, avoidance, denial, or just feeling like a victim. They can become so entrenched that they become what we do and who we are.

Whichever pattern you experience, ask yourself this simple question. Are your strategies working? How long does the effect of the emotional trigger last? A moment? All day?

Here is a simple technique; I used it this morning:

When you become aware that something is slowly but surely eating you up from the inside, simply stop and face it; challenge it to do its worst. With the lingering worry I had this morning I just sat and gave the feeling 100% of my attention and invited it to go right ahead and destroy me. It almost instantly dissolved.

I don't know if this will always work for everyone, but my personal experience is that we have reserves of strength and resilience that far exceed most of what our emotional demons can match.

Of course, building that inner strength is the key. And, surprise, surprise: regular mindfulness meditation is the best way to build that strength!

Why generosity is a giveaway

It is Christmas as I write this, and here we all are, spending money on unnecessary things for people who don't need them, while half the planet starves or gets bombed. Does this rankle you, as it does me? I may be an old bore, but Christmas keeps challenging me more and more. I find that it really rubs at an old sore of guilt and a realisation of the limits of my compassionate action.

I've told people that I don't want any presents, but I'll get some anyway. Really I neither need nor want a single thing (unless someone has a free skiing week going, in which case please stop reading now and email me immediately!).

But the thing this guilt brings up is the whole challenge of generosity, and what we can infer about our need to hold on to what we consider to be ours. And also why this holds us back from spiritual freedom.

The tradition of Buddhist teaching is that there is no 'fee' for the teaching. The student donates what he or she can. This creates discomfort for us Westerners, who are used to paying for things with a fixed price set by the seller. When we're asked to pay what we feel something is worth, it gets difficult. What actually happens in the West for meditation teachers doing this is that they get paid peanuts. For a day's retreat for example, people may contribute a tenner. Compare that with the fee for one hour with a therapist or a day of professional development, where we'll pay anything between £40 for an hour to £500 for a day.

Why is that? I don't think it relates to perceived value. I have to admit that when I'm asked to donate, I get mean. It presents a direct challenge to the concept of 'me' and 'mine'. We're so stuck in the culture of materialism and money, and governed by the whole concept of our separateness (from the world and from others), that anything that erodes what seems to be 'ours' is perceived as a full frontal attack. To let things go willingly is a form of suicide.

How might we deepen our meditation practice to begin healing this frantic grasping, get a bit closer to finding the intense stillness and spaciousness that is just under the surface? If you wanted to wrap up the whole of this teaching in two words, they would be, 'let go'. That means letting go of the tight hold we have on the stuff we consider ours, as if we can take it with us when we die.

Essentially, we are naked. I'm no naturist, especially in Wales in December, but I do know that when I hit the sweet spot of naked awareness in meditation, there's no 'me' and no 'mine', and that it feels like the most abundant place in the world.

Generosity helps us let go. When we're being generous and selfless, the 'me' part that defends what's 'ours' takes a nap. And then we get a huge surprise: being generous and kind makes us feel good. Win blooming win!

My challenge to you, and to myself, is this. Today, tomorrow and every day for the next week, do three generous things. They only count if they make you feel uncomfortable! Just sending £5 to charity with your phone is not good enough. The acts must require you to let go of your holding on to the idea of things and money as 'mine' and, by inference, part of 'me'. Get creative. Try harder. Lighten up.

Also, because I know you're all good mindfulness practitioners who sit every morning, you can make this easy. Simply make some kind of promise at the start of the day. Repeat it aloud three times. Imagine yourself doing it. Imagine how you will feel doing the generous things you're going to do. Imagine what you will say to yourself on doing them.

(By the way, sending a bag of single-estate shade-grown organic heritage-varietal fair-trade artisan-roasted coffee to your meditation teacher is officially the most generous act of all, and can lead to immediate enlightenment).

How to clear your head when things get mad-busy

Most of us know the feeling: there's too much to do, we're under pressure; we feel like a rabbit frozen in the headlights. Things get cloudy, our normal capacity to function efficiently goes out the window, and we resort to doing what's easy rather than what's needed. Or, if it gets worse, we're in a panic attack.

Why is this? Chemistry. As your amygdala recognises a threatening situation, the hypothalamus and pituitary glands send signals to adrenal glands and you get a cortisol boost (which can stay in your body all day). Your frontal cortex gets suppressed so you can't think straight. Sensitivity to new pressure increases. Ouch!

So what can you do about it? You can **STOP**. This is an acronym. Let's look at it.

S is for stopping. Invest a minute in your mental health. If you continue in the stress cycle, things may get worse, or you'll just hang on and have an inefficient, unhappy day. So pause, and employ an emergency mindfulness technique described fully in my online Taster course (website link at the back of the book) - in essence the instruction is to breathe mindfully, with a longer out-breath, smile, and feel your feet on the ground; this will reset your parasympathetic nervous system.

T is for taking care. Your employer, your client and your family need you to be healthy and at your best. Taking care of yourself is a good investment for everyone. You know what works for you – take a walk, have a positive chat, do yoga, (but don't gorge on sugar and coffee or the stress will come back). Top tip: be kind to someone else. It makes you feel happy. Forgive yourself, drop the self-criticism, have compassion for this human that is you.

O is for organise. There's plenty of self-management advice out there so I may not be the best to advise. But from 35 years of consultancy, here's what works for me. First, I create a spreadsheet with a row for each task. Then I add columns for urgency, dependencies (what else do you need, from whom / where / when), and a practical task list. Or use a good app like Todoist. When you're clear, let others know when the tasks can be delivered, and do not succumb to bullying. You know best what's possible. You are a human, not a machine. Be polite and assertive.

P is for pausing. Yes, again. And again. And more. Before you zoom off into 'doing' mode, remember the state you were in before you **stop**ped and how you got there. Commit to checking-in with your mental wellbeing at least once an hour with a one minute pause – time for 'being'.

I hope that helps.

The Way of Un

Now it is January. The holiday season is behind us. Our lovely guest has gone. This weekend it was time to disassemble the guest bed in the practice room. It's held together with 8 bolts. In case you think I'm way off track, I'll come back to this later, and why it led to an insight for my teaching.

I'm teaching mindfulness, it seems. But really, mindfulness is just an approach, though a critical one, on the path to something. What's driving us, and where are we going? Why do we practise? Is it just to get a bit calmer, to learn how to deal better with stress or difficult relationships? Those are all good reasons, but is it possible we are we seeking something deeper?

If you're not quite sure where the practice is going, but something keeps you coming back for more, or you feel that there is more to discover about life, you're on the path to Awakening.

In fact it is a healthier approach to just keep practising without a specific goal, since having a goal becomes just another hurdle to get over. Awakening is much faster when you simply relax into the present, into how things are, without trying to get anywhere, achieve anything, or become something other than what you are, now.

Now this is where nuts and bolts come in. As I unscrewed the nuts on the bed frame, it became clear that the moment when the nut comes off the thread is unpredictable. There you are, just turning the nut, and all of a sudden it comes off. It takes no more effort to make that last turn than any other part of the process. In fact a hard wrench of the spanner might damage the thread.

Practice is like this. It's most effective with a light touch. Think of a fluffy feather falling slowly to the ground. It takes no effort for it to float downwards, and it will inexorably fall, ever so gently until, at some point it comes to rest on the ground.

I like to call this the Way of Un. The Way of Un is the approach of making the least effort possible. Any verb you can think of indicates too much striving. Relaxing, breathing, letting go, experiencing – they are all far too active! Even to say 'do nothing' has got that 'doing' thing in there.

Un, as a prefix, seems to nicely sum up the negation of something – undoing, unlimited, undressed, unhappy, unravel, unrestricted.

All the usual meditation techniques, like watching the breath, body awareness and so on, are great. They are a critical part of the training, and a support, especially for busy minds. But their purpose is to take us to a place where we can even let those practices go.

So next time you practise, try the Way of Un! Just be aware of whether you are making any effort whatsoever. If you are, Un it. Just let it go, relax more, until there is nothing but what is. And when you touch that moment, you will know that it is unknowable.

The secret of practice: don't

Hi. I've just walked back home from collecting an overnight bag from my daughter's friend, where she did a sleepover. It is a few hours before the Wales England match, when my concentration will be at its highest. However, on the walk back I dropped into a deep Un-practice, which may be helpful to share.

This is essentially about how to put the Way of Un into practice, and its amazing power. The instruction is so simple you may miss me saying it:

'Stay awake and do nothing'.

In particular, drop any goals. Do not:

- Practise to get calm
- Practise to get enlightened
- Practise to become a better human being
- Think about what you're doing or its effect
- Change anything

Just stay attentive to the nowness.

Leave it alone.

Get out of the way.

These simple practices are about allowing your natural capacity for awareness to do the experiencing for you. It's just like breathing at night; you go to sleep trusting that your body will keep you breathing. So it is with natural, naked awareness. You do nothing but stay awake to what's happening.

Practising in this way, with no striving for an outcome, can lead to great bliss. Be wary of bliss, by the way, as it can easily take you off into lala land where you suddenly think that you are fully enlightened and how wonderful people will think you are, and so on.

If bliss arises, just experience it and see how it changes. If sadness or an itch arises, just experience it and see how it changes.

That's it, short and sweet.

Why your demons are your friends

Ok so there you are on the cushion or on retreat and hoping to have a blissfully calm meditation when, quite suddenly, it all goes pear-shaped. You feel like someone has just punched you in the stomach, or you feel all shaky, hot and bothered, or perhaps as heavy as lead.

'What the heck is this?' you ask. That's a good question, and you may or may not get an answer. Sometimes there's a clear insight, like 'Oh my god, I do this all the time and don't even notice' or 'this is just how I felt when I lost that contract.' But at other times we simply can't pin it down.

The fact is that mindfulness opens up and loosens up holdings-on that may have been present for many years. Just creating the open space for this to happen is rare and precious. But we have to be prepared for 'unpleasant' experiences. They are actually more valuable and useful to our ongoing growth than the bliss states.

This happens in particular with bodywork, hence the importance of physical movement and the exploration of body sensations as part of the practice. Our bodies hold responses to trauma.

For me, being a mild mannered fellow, I can bottle up anger and I almost never shout. Then, during a body scan, or 30 minutes into sitting meditation, I will suddenly notice the tension in my throat.

When you purposefully allow the tension to be experienced, it is like releasing a floodgate of held emotion. At this point you might burst into tears or laugh out loud.

Or perhaps we hold tension in our belly whenever we're in a stressful environment like in a meeting. So when we purposefully connect with the feelings in the belly and relax, we may find something loosens and opens up and we become more open-hearted and open-minded.

Such experiences may be initially unpleasant, but they can be of great value. In daily life they will inform us quickly when something is wrong and needs to be dealt with. For example, in the case of an overbearing boss, the next time your he/she behaves badly you may notice the suppressed tension coming in your throat but, with the insight gained earlier, instead of following your old pattern of internalising the stress you take that energy and direct it to - respectfully, but assertively - challenge the boss's behaviour. Or when you next notice your belly getting tense in a meeting, you take it as an early warning system that something is going on that needs to be addressed and challenged.

Your body is far quicker to pick up these cues than your thinking brain. In fact the body is the most effective tool we have for developing emotional intelligence.

So, when these more challenging feelings come in our practice, welcome them. What may at first appear to be demons are actually friends - friends who keep trying to contact you. If you're too busy to make time to listen they eventually get tetchy and slap you in the face. Have patience, hear what they're saying, and reflect on what they're pointing to.

Why being LALA is better than going doolally

Pausing is one of the most poignant and illuminating exercises in this whole game of awakening.

When we pause, we deliberately face what's just below the surface. I first noticed this in the car. My habit was (and is) to reach for the big knobbly on button on the radio the moment I take off. God forbid that I should be present and undistracted for even one second! Having become aware of the habit I now try to remember to hold off pressing the button. And mostly what I find, in that moment of naked awareness, is some kind of dissatisfaction. Mostly it's just a low rumble, but it's enough to subconsciously motivate me to turn on the radio.

Meeting this underlying dissatisfaction can be highly uncomfortable. We notice a kind of undertow, a hidden and somewhat malevolent-feeling force stirring underneath, but however much we splash around on the surface, it remains. It is not anything too traumatic, we're neither depressed nor anxious, but the undercurrent is there.

The objective is not to get rid of the lurking discomfort, but rather to recognise that the drivers of our behaviour in everyday life run deep, and they have a lot to tell us.

So I came up with LALA. I tried to turn it into Doolally, as an acronym, but I thought people might not take me seriously, so LALA it is!

The first **L stands for listen.** That's the point where you don't turn on the radio, or where one of your stress triggers kicks in and if you're lucky you see it coming. So you turn up the awareness and tune-in with fearless attention.

Next comes **A for acceptance**. Whatever you feel, whatever comes to mind, you just let it be as it is. Feel it working through you. No comment, no judgement.

Having encountered the feelings and emotions, and recognised their strength and effect, you're now ready for the second **L, which stands for learn.** Now we can employ cognitive intelligence to recognise what's going on, and to perhaps choose a more functional response.

The final **A is for action** or, more accurately, appropriate action, where we consciously make a wholesome response rather than unthinking one.

That can all happen in space of a few seconds, but what an amazing and speedy journey we've taken, and one which can, in my experience, entirely divert the course of the day into a more positive direction. It's like putting a pebble in the course of the stream right at the spring, which may send the water off to become a river in quite a different valley.

That can happen in the space of a passing moment. How much more can we learn from grabbing five or fifteen minutes to deliberately meditate before we reach for our favourite, zombie-like distraction?

Personally, I'd rather be LALA than doolally.

Recognising stress habits

We all have different ways of reacting to stress. It's important to recognise the state that you're in. List out the indicators that you notice in yourself, when stress is beginning to take over.

For example, you might experience a compulsion to try to do more in a shorter space of time. It could be that you have particular physical symptoms such as getting hot, a sense of irritation, the beginning of a headache, tightness in the stomach or the jaw and so on. It could show up by not sleeping well. Identify your signs of stress and get them down on paper.

After noticing how stress plays out for you, and noting the signs, the next task is to recognise what you do when the stress arrives. Perhaps you just push even harder, getting your head down and putting on the blinkers. There may be a sense narrowing the focus of your attention. It may be that you adopt mind-numbing activities such as web-surfing, doing mundane tasks, or avoiding facing the issues that are causing the stress by making another cup of coffee, over-eating, under-eating, self-medicating, or talking with others as if they can magically resolve the issue for you.

Simply by becoming familiar with both your indicators of stress and your reactions, you are already well on the road towards unravelling habits which may have built up over a lifetime, you might start to be less of a slave to your bad habits.

So, having noted your indicators and reactions around stress, now it's time to establish new ways to react when you notice the stress appearing.

At this point it's useful to be clear about the kinds of activity that we know are effective for us in reducing stress. Again, for each of us this will be different.
Some of the most common helpful approaches for de-escalating the stress response include:

- Physical exercise. This might simply mean getting up and walking around a little, swinging your arms, or stretching.
- Fresh air. Getting outdoors for a breath of fresh air can quickly change the physical stress reaction.
- Talk to someone about something else.
- Listen to music.
- Tidy up.
- Take time to really savour the smell of a flower, a good coffee or a nourishing snack.

It's useful to actually make a list of the kinds of activities that you know are nourishing and refreshing for you.

Try to create some new habits, whereby you employ these techniques intentionally when your stress indicators appear. The new habits may feel clunky at first, as you're in the process of challenging your brain's normal reactions. But stick with it for at least a week and see if it's effective and getting easier.

Build on the positives and observe the results.

Making mindfulness a lifelong practice

Mindfulness is out there. There are mindfulness colouring books, mindfulness T shirts and mindfulness retreats that are really pampering sessions. It's all good, but much of it is a shallow interpretation of the practice and is unlikely to be life-changing.

For those who want to go deeper, there's sure to be an 8-week course locally. But it seems that many who complete the course don't keep on with the practice. It stays theoretical. It fades. And then they're back with the same old worries and stresses and making the same mistakes again and again.

So I want to make the case for plugging away at the practice, and making it a lifetime's work, because changing habits and becoming happier needs on-going work at the roots of our being.

I'd like to share the story of my own journey in this practice and some key lessons I've learned from this.

My first couple of years were with a mindful movement teacher who taught a kind of free range Tai Chi. I didn't realise it, but it this was a great place to start. Body awareness is a very effective way to by-pass the thinking mind and connect with raw experience. So I recommend yoga, Tai Chi, or a similar practice alongside meditation.

The next step on my journey was studying Buddha Dharma under an eclectic and perhaps eccentric Canadian teacher who had studied in the Burmese Forest Tradition and been ordained as Anandabodhi. Some years later he was recognized by the 16th Karmapa and the Dalai Lama as fully enlightened.

To sit in front of him was to sit in the room with a mountain.

Some of his students are now amazing teachers themselves. There is an energetic and mind-to-mind connection with a teacher who has deep realisation of the nature of mind. Settle for nothing less. We may be inspired by books, but we need a skilled teacher.

The next point is simple: don't give up, and do whatever helps most to keep your energy and interest high. Find the way to practice that suits your personality; it will be different for you than for me. For example some people are much better moving than sitting, some are better with quiet whilst some learn most with sounds around them.

It's helpful too when life gets difficult! My cosy life has had some real challenges. It's by road-testing the practice when it matters most, that the biggest learning comes about. I'm not recommending that you go and look for trouble, but I am saying that when there are difficulties in your life, that's actually the best time for practice. *'Start where you are'*, as Pema Chodron suggests.

Finally there's the need for good motivation. It's really important to be clear why you're doing this and what your intention is. Whist you may start with wanting to do something about your own happiness, and that's important, the practice will only develop deeply if your aspiration becomes selfless. When you really want to help others and contribute to a better world, it actually opens up channels of insight. And you may also have read that the happiest mind-state is compassion, so that's a win-win scenario.

With all the suffering in the world, there's plenty of opportunity to practise! We probably can't change what happening in war zones, but if we can take a more compassionate view towards what's right in front our nose, and enough of us do that, the world will change.

If you need a big idea to work with, how about healing the world, starting here?

How to hold a mindful conversation

Mindful listening is a key skill for coaches and other 'listening' professionals, but it's also a core workplace skill for all of us. Mindful listening helps nurture better interactions, speeds up the process of understanding other points of view and leads to more effective solutions and productivity.

When we hold a conversation, whose voice do we really listen to? That of the person we're talking to, or the narrative in our own head?

How fast do we jump to conclusions, make judgments or form opinions, find answers to someone else's problems, or just get bored and drift off?

"You cannot truly listen to anyone and do anything else at the same time," said *Scott Peck.*

The core skill in getting listening right is *selfless attention.*

The 'selfless' part of this approach is critical, and may require a real change of stance on our part. Most of us react and respond quickly and automatically to things we hear, interrupting in our heads before the other person has finished speaking. As humans we're programmed to be very sensitive to what we think is bad news or a threat, and we therefore react quickly to anything that seems like a challenge to 'me' or my views. Our own emotions and reactions hold us back from focusing fully on what the other person is saying.

The 'attention' part is about being fully attentive and receptive about what is being said and how it's being said. This means tuning in with all our receptive skills; feeling how reactions are forming in the body, and using our intuition. These other ways of tuning-in pick up cues from body language, read nuances in the other person's emotions, and help us become aware of what's not being said. Or, as *Peter Drucker* puts it:

"The most important thing in communication is hearing what isn't said."

Mindfulness training gives us some of the core skills we need here. In particular, learning how to focus, concentrate, and listen with non-judging awareness. We also learn to tune-in to the body's wisdom, recognising the signs that are personal to each of us, such as tightening of the throat.

When we hold a mindful conversation, we give the other person as much space, time and attention as they need to communicate fully with us. Nothing we do should stop their flow of thought or speech.

In fact, we should aim to develop active listening skills and relevant questioning, so that the other person is encouraged to express themselves unreservedly, and to think on their feet.

The most potent tool we can employ in mindful listening is to do nothing, be patient, and wait silently.

Silence can be awkward, but what may feel like a gap to us may be a creative and important moment for the other person. If they're forming an insight, time stands still. When they are ready to articulate what's been forming, they will. Our job is to give them the space for this to happen. This is not a passive role for us. In creating this space, we give the other person permission to make a creative leap in their own understanding.

We are social animals, and how we communicate with others is a key skill that affects many aspects of our lives. Get this right and see how your relationships change. Mindful listening also offers us an opportunity to bring key mindfulness skills, such as patience and kindness, into daily life.

Mindfulness through breathing

Perhaps the most fundamental and most practised form of meditation is breathing mindfully. Simply by observing the movement and nature of our own breathing, we can train ourselves to concentrate, relax, and develop equanimity toward whatever comes our way.

It sounds incredibly simple, and it is. One of the advantages of using breathing as a tool in developing mindfulness, is that it's always available to us. Breathing brings mind and body together.

Humans and seals are unique in the animal kingdom, having the choice of breathing automatically or intentionally. Other animals have one or the other. Whales for example only breathe intentionally, when they surface for air, whilst dogs pant without any intentional control. For the most part human breathing goes on automatically, thanks to our parasympathetic nervous system. However, we can also choose to hold, lengthen, or shorten the breath.

This facility makes mindful breathing particularly interesting. When we put our attention on the breathing, and just sit and observe, we actually find that every breath is subtly unique, and therefore continually interesting.

With breathing as the object of our attention, calm naturally arises, and with that we can see how scattered the mind can be and how elusive full concentration really is. We may also notice the tendency to judge what's happening around us, or in our thoughts. This is not bad. It is normal. But it's a great insight simply to notice the distractibility of our minds, and the way we unthinkingly categorise events and thoughts, crudely, as good or bad.

Mindful breathing exercises are very simple, and form the foundation work at all stages of mindfulness training. Wherever you are, whatever you are doing, you have access to practise attentiveness to the breath.

A simple instruction for mindful breathing is available at the end of the book.

Mindfulness through hearing

Our perception of the world is highly skewed to visual stimuli. However, it's important to realise that what we think we see, is mostly made up in our brains from pattern recognition and memory, so that what comes in through the eyes is really just a trigger for the picture which forms in our mind.

With all the senses, there is this tendency for the brain to try to piece things together, making informed guesses on the basis of sometimes-scant information then jumping to conclusions! However, with some senses, smelling and hearing in particular, we have more opportunity to train ourselves to just notice the raw data before it gets processed.

The essence of these exercises is to experience the raw data, the sounds, simply as sounds, without judgement.

For example, if we hear a throaty rumble outside the window then the normal sequence is that we categorise this, for example as a motorbike, then form a positive or negative emotional response, that we have learned to associate with motorbikes. In mindful hearing, we simply hear the sound, full stop. It comes, it changes, and it's gone; no analysis is required.

Mindfulness exercises that focus on hearing, or on smell for example, can therefore be very useful in a number of ways. First of all they help us to stay finely tuned into the present moment, as long as we avoid analysis of the raw data. They also train us to tune in to our body's wisdom and, thirdly, they help build the capacity for sustained concentration. Finally they help us recognise our tendency to create stories of our own making from very little real fact.

A mindful hearing exercise is included at the end of the book.

Mindfulness in the body

In a busy, active environment we mostly live in our heads. We drag our body around like a faithful dog, taking its miraculous physiology for granted, and only really notice our body when things go wrong and we experience discomfort, pain, or illness.

Yet our bodies are the most incredibly sensitive instruments and, in many ways, a much better gauge of our emotional life than our busy minds.

It can come as a surprise to some people to be told that the key tool in developing mindfulness is to tune-in to our bodies. In fact the normal way we approach new skills, by thinking it through, is specifically to be avoided. Dealing with difficult emotions, for example, can be addressed much more quickly by tuning-in to the sensations in our body. In fact trying to resolve difficult thoughts by thinking alone, will often lead to more confusion. Our gut feeling is to be trusted!

By becoming more aware of body sensations, externally and internally, we can access an incredible reserve of emotional intelligence. Most of us need to train to get out of our heads so much, and back into our bodies.

It is a great way to relax. If you suffer from poor sleep patterns it can really help, but try to keep awake while you're doing it. Not only is it an exercise in tuning into the body, it's also about developing the capacity for sustained attention.

It's good advice too, to stretch, do yoga or have a walk before your formal sitting practice. This movement in the body gives you a better chance of movement in the mind.

The body scan exercise is described at the end of the book.

How to be happy

Can we be happy, with less effort? Can we do this in a way that helps others at the same time?

We're all seeking happiness. We use up enormous amounts of energy trying to adjust and control our environment to make ourselves feel happy - or at least to avoid discomfort. This driving force sees us planning and fantasising our futures, and regretting (or celebrating) what has already happened.

We think that if we get better at generating the nice things, and smarter at avoiding the bad things, the result will be more happiness. If we can get a better job, with a nicer boss and a bigger income, stay fit, get a better house, a better relationship, nice clothes, a nice car, then all will be well. If we can insulate ourselves from upset and secure our pension, all will be well.

Does that really work? Well, if it does, we're all in trouble. Seeking happiness from the outside, the drive for 'more' and 'better' uses up natural as well as emotional resources. It also separates us from one another, because the sense of a limited pot of resources will create winners and losers. Life becomes a battleground.

Just look around, and see if the 'get more' approach is working. We all have more stuff, in this country anyway, but we're suffering more anxiety and depression than ever before. Our kids are not happy, and the planet is in trouble. Doh! We all know this, yet we keep banging our heads against the wall.

Materialism and competition do not create happiness. Agreed, a certain level of basic needs must be met; the need for food, shelter, safety is a matter of survival. Beyond that, we may get a quick high from the latest i-phone or shot of flavoured vodka, or feel we've 'made it' when we see a certain number on our bank statement. But those things are temporary and the more we assign value to them, the more tightly we get bound up in this spider's web of delusion.

There is nothing inherently wrong in possessions. Nor is there anything inherently good about poverty. The problem is the value we assign to having and to not having; the way we hold on tightly to the things that we like, and avoid the things we don't like.

So the root of unhappiness lies in how we make judgements about whether something is good or bad in the first place. It's a challenge, because our brain's neural pathways have learned and embodied our views before we are even aware of those views. We've hardwired our responses.

Messages from our parents, teachers, advertisers, bloggers, friends, colleagues, Google, and the rest of our experience, keep reinforcing our pre-dispositions. It takes a lot of guts to think differently with this bombardment of messages all day long - especially when we measure success by totalling the net worth of our externalities such as material goods or positive relationships.

If we really want to create contentment for ourselves, and to generate positive impacts for other people and the planet, we need to understand the nature of suffering itself, and the principle of cause and effect. We need to understand, and experience, mental freedom.

This is a lifetime's work. There is no quick fix! So I'm inviting you to join me, and many others, in this exploration. For me, one indicator of success is if I can help others. So let me lay out the basics here.

The first thing to note is that what we consider to be real, is just our experience, as processed in the brain. A great example is happening right now, in the room where I am writing this. There is a fly buzzing in the room, and before I can think 'fly', my body reacts with an 'unpleasant' tone. It's not the fly's fault. It was my experience that put the fly in the 'bad' category. This happened for a reason. There was a cause and there was its effect. We could postulate many theories for the cause, but that may or may not be useful. The important lesson here is that suffering is personal. We create it out of otherwise neutral phenomena. And the same is true of pleasant experience, with few exceptions.

So the first part of alleviating suffering is to realise that it's all about how we respond, and that a lifetime of learning that has created automatic reactions to things that arise.

Pain, as an example, can be managed very effectively with mindfulness, when we learn to separate out the physical symptom from our reaction to it (read *Burch* et al).

The next part of alleviating suffering relates to the issue of separateness. As long as we see ourselves as independent beings, alone and self-reliant, we naturally seek to protect ourselves. The fact is that we are not separate, we are just one short-lived iteration of the human genome; a miraculous assembly of carbon, hydrogen, oxygen and minerals in the soup of life, and we are entirely dependent on and supported by the rest of the soup.

Kindness and compassion illustrate this dependency. Take care of the rest of the ingredients, and the soup will taste better. When you're kind, you will be happier.

The third part to overcoming suffering is to become more aware of when our minds are being driven by the poisonous emotions of greed, hatred and delusion in particular. These mind states can become the way we deal with our sense of separateness.

Let's take a mundane example – the mobile phone. We buy a better model, maybe because it works a little better, or because we want to look cool, or because the phone provider is feeding our greed with very clever marketing. Whatever the outward reason, the desire for something other than what is present is described as greed in the classical texts. Next we get a brief and unskilful text from a colleague, which we interpret as blaming us for some failure. We immediately go on the defensive and send back a sharp reply. Pushing away what we don't want is one description of hatred. Later, when we check our latest Facebook post and see that we have only three likes, we get depressed and imagine that everyone hates us. This confused reaction to something we imagine is delusion.

Greed, hatred and delusion; the trio that drives suffering and the creation of our own mind.

So where do we start with this mammoth task of reprogramming ourselves, our perceptions and our reactions to those perceptions? Contrary to much popular belief about mindfulness and self-improvement, the real starting point is good ethics. In the traditional training for a Buddhist monk, the first stage is to commit to being truthful, caring for all life, being non-violent in personal relationships, and letting go of greed. Meditation comes later. In fact generosity alone can be a path to mental liberation. No need to sit on a cushion and chant 'om'.

Words cannot adequately describe mental freedom. The only way we will understand this is through our own direct experience. But here are two clues:

First, it only happens in the Now.

Secondly, it's within us and dependent on nothing at all. That's why we have to learn and practise being present. When you experience the transcendental, even for an instant, you will know that every word here is true.

There is a lot to learn and a lot to practise to sort this out. An eight-week mindfulness course is a great start, but the re-programming is on-going. So here is one thing you can do, starting now, that is going to speed up the whole process: *be kind*. Yes, it is that simple.

Making it happen, easily

Many people have good intentions to do the mindfulness practices, and know it makes sense to, but then find the day just seems to go by without it happening.

There are some common reasons for not getting started, or not keeping it going. Luckily there are also some easy fixes!

First of all is **intention**. If one's motivation is strong and clear, then space for practice just opens up. Therefore it is important to clarify and be sure why you want to practise. If the intention is to become happier, that's great and an important starting place. But if it's only about your happiness, the energy will fade. When the motivation is to benefit all living beings and the health of the planet, and when you get to see that by setting this intention at the start of each day opportunities present themselves to fulfil this goal, confidence increases and the energy for practice builds.

Next we need to look at **habits**. We are such creatures of habit that our days are largely mapped out before we even get out of bed. We can use this to advantage. Simply schedule in 5 minutes sometime in the getting up schedule. For instance the getting up routine includes pee, shower, dress, eat breakfast. It isn't difficult to add a five minute practise session between two of those activities. Set your new schedule, paste big notes on the bedroom and bathroom walls, and slavishly do it, every day. If you've got time to shower you've got time to practise. After 30 days it will get easier and after 60 days it will be as natural as breathing.

It's a win-win to **bring mindfulness into the things you already do.** For example, why not brush your teeth, empty the bins, drink your coffee, and greet colleagues with mindful attention. Even if your mindfulness is just there for a moment, you will find yourself doing it more often and more readily.

When starting, **find a practice that suits you**. Mindful breathing is always a good place to start. But there are simple alternatives including mindful listening, or you may find it easier to bring these exercises into movement, such as walking. Others may find that the body scan comes most easily. Start with what works for you, and when your habit is building, challenge yourself to explore other mindfulness practices.

There's another important point. It's that **any state of mind or circumstance is an opportunity to learn more about ourselves**, so practice is possible whatever's going on. We may feel discomfort, reluctance or seek distraction from unpleasant feelings, but if we can be just a little disciplined, and patient with the discomfort, there can be great insights to be found from difficult states of mind, or even from simply from drilling down into what we're really feeling when we don't feel like practising.

Mindfulness exercises

Instructions for mindfulness with breathing

First establish good posture. Whether you're sitting on a chair, or on a cushion, you need to maintain an upright and reasonably straight spine, with your head resting naturally balanced. Your hands can rest comfortably on your lap or on your knees, so that there is no strain on the shoulders.

To begin with, it will be easier to close your eyes, although as you become more practised, you will find that keeping the eyes open is important. Be aware that with your eyes closed you may get sleepy, so if you feel this happening open them. With the eyes open, you may get too distracted. In that case half close the eyes and let your gaze rest on the floor.

When you feel comfortable and settled, you simply bring your attention to the breathing. Do not try to change the breath in any way. This is not a yoga exercise. Simply notice as much as you can about the sensation of breathing.

For example you could simply notice the movement of in breath and out breath: how long and deep are they? Are they regular or irregular? Does the air feel hot or cold? You can focus your attention at the nostrils where the air comes in and out, or at the lungs, or on the movement of the torso and belly. It doesn't really matter exactly what you focus on, but whatever it is that you choose, stay with that only.

It is perfectly natural for the mind to wander off. When it does, observe the wandering with interest, not criticism. As soon as you are aware that you have lost concentration, simply bring your attention back to the breathing.

Try to keep your attention on the unfolding of the present. Just notice if you have started thinking of events in the past or of possible future events and, if you do drift backwards or forwards in time, just come back to now, without criticism.

If just focusing on the breath is challenging, try one of these supports:

- Count the breaths, say up to 7, and back again to 1
- Say to yourself 'breathing in' on the in–breath, and 'letting go' on the out-breath

Instructions for mindfulness while listening

In your sitting posture, come to a point of comfort and stability.

Then simply listen to sounds close by, followed by those in the neighbourhood, and then far away sounds. Notice every little sound.

Notice the tendency for the mind to classify what the sound belongs to, then make it into a story (ah… that sound is a motorbike, he's in a tearing rush, what an idiot, he could kill a child, like Annie next door, who's probably walking home now…). So see if you can listen without that happening.

Notice also, any tendency to let your ears or mind linger on the sound. Just let it go as soon as it's over.

Again, it is perfectly natural for the mind to wander off. Do not judge this as bad. If you've noticed it happen you've learned a lot. Simply come back to the mindfulness exercise.

When you've spent some time listening to the sounds, bring your attention to the gaps between the sounds

Instructions for the body scan

It is very important that you set aside at least 20 minutes for this exercise, and ideally 30. You must be in a place where you are comfortable and undisturbed. You will need a yoga mat or a folded over blanket to lie on, and a small cushion for your head.

Lie on your back with your hands lying by the side of your body or resting gently on your belly. Begin by making contact with the breathing, gently bringing your attention to the full experience of the in-breath and of the out-breath. You may be able to notice your abdomen moving up and down with the rhythm of the breath.

You then bring your attention to the top of the head and simply notice what you can feel. Notice the actual sensations of hot or cold, texture, tingling, achiness, whatever it is that you experience. You are looking for the direct experience, without needing to put words to the sensations.

Once you have fully taken in the experience of sensation at the top of the head, you can move the focus down to your face. You can break this down further into forehead, cheeks, chin, eyes, ears, nose, lips and so on.

Continue this process, slowly and gradually, right down through every part of the body, on the external surfaces, and whatever you can feel of what is going on inside the body such as breathing, heart beat, gurgling in the gut, and so on. Take the scan right down to your toes.

After you have scanned right through the body, try to become aware of the body as a whole. Simply experience being a human organism, alive and sensing, with nothing to do.

This body scan is simply an exploration, and an exercise in concentrated awareness of body sensation. Try to avoid making comments or judgements, such as 'this feels good' or 'that feels bad'.

If you find that you're beginning to fall asleep, keep your eyes open and see if you can 'fall awake'. Conversely if you find yourself distracted, keep the eyes closed, return to the breathing, and maybe take the cushion away.

Instructions for the '10 second re-boot'

This is a one of the practices I teach beginners in my Taster course, as it can quickly de-stress you when you need it most.

Start as with mindful breathing, just experiencing the natural rhythm of the breath.

But in this practice you focus on the outbreath, making it noticeably longer and deeper and slower. Let the in-breath do what is naturally does.

As you exhale, let go of tension. Just relax, more and more. You can say to yourself 'letting go'.

To super-charge this practice, do two more things:

1. Smile – just put a smile on your face and in your belly.

2. Bring attention to your feet and feel yourself connecting to the ground.

What to do next

I hope this book has been useful. I've loved writing the articles. For me, the path of mindfulness has led here, to my surprise. It's a much better place than the one I inhabited in my earlier years.

If you're new to mindfulness or you just dip in and out of apps and articles, I strongly recommend that you take an 8 week course. The daily practice over two months can be transformative. Make sure the teacher has long meditation experience.

If you've done an 8 week course, the challenge is to keep it going. Find ways to integrate the practices into everyday activities. Try to make even a 5 minute practice time every morning and set a simple intention, such as 'I will be kind in all my interactions today'.

If you want to explore your mind more deeply, and get to the roots of suffering, retreats are critical. Find a teacher with deep experience who you trust.

I offer online courses and remote coaching through my website Mindfulwork.co.uk, with a focus on bringing mindfulness into the workplace. You can sign up to my newsletter too, and I'll invite you to webinars, retreats and other ways to keep the practice fresh, interesting and relevant.

Be well, be happy,

Simon